People that Changed the Course of History

The Story of
Andrew Jackson
250 Years After His Birth

Danielle Thorne

People that Changed the Course of History:
The Story of Andrew Jackson 250 Years After His Birth

Website: www.atlantic-pub.com • Email: sales@atlantic-pub.com
SAN Number: 268-1250

Library of Congress Cataloging-in-Publication Data

Names: Thorne, Danielle, author.
Title: People that changed the course of history : the story of Andrew
    Jackson 250 years after his birth / by Danielle Thorne.
Other titles: Story of Andrew Jackson 250 years after his birth
Description: Ocala, Florida : Atlantic Publishing Group, Inc., 2016. |
    Includes bibliographical references and index.
Identifiers: LCCN 2016036837| ISBN 9781620231463 (alk. paper) | ISBN
    1620231468 (alk. paper) | ISBN 9781620232279 (alk. paper)
Subjects: LCSH: Jackson, Andrew, 1767-1845. | Presidents--United
    States--Biography.
Classification: LCC E382 .T48 2016 | DDC 973.5/6092 [B] --dc23 LC record
available at https://lccn.loc.gov/2016036837

PROJECT MANAGER: Rebekah Sack – rsack@atlantic-pub.com
ASSISTANT EDITOR: Taylor Centers – gtcenters@gmail.com
INTERIOR LAYOUT AND JACKET DESIGN: Janine Milstrey – j.milstrey@red-cape.de
COVER DESIGN: Jackie Miller – sullmill@charter.net

Printed in the United States

Reduce. Reuse.
RECYCLE.

A decade ago, Atlantic Publishing signed the Green Press Initiative. These guidelines promote environmentally friendly practices, such as using recycled stock and vegetable-based inks, avoiding waste, choosing energy-efficient resources, and promoting a no-pulping policy. We now use 100-percent recycled stock on all our books. The results: in one year, switching to post-consumer recycled stock saved 24 mature trees, 5,000 gallons of water, the equivalent of the total energy used for one home in a year, and the equivalent of the greenhouse gases from one car driven for a year.

Over the years, we have adopted a number of dogs from rescues and shelters. First there was Bear and after he passed, Ginger and Scout. Now, we have Kira, another rescue. They have brought immense joy and love not just into our lives, but into the lives of all who met them.

We want you to know a portion of the profits of this book will be donated in Bear, Ginger and Scout's memory to local animal shelters, parks, conservation organizations, and other individuals and nonprofit organizations in need of assistance.

– Douglas & Sherri Brown,
President & Vice-President of Atlantic Publishing

ANDREW JACKSON

Contents

Introduction: A Sword to the Face

Two young boys creep through the underbrush of the wild South Carolina woods hiding from cavalry regiments of the enemy. They call them the British Dragoons. The revolutionary war has been raging for four years now, and after escaping an attack on their town, the boys have survived for three days without any food or rest. Andrew and Robert Jackson, have no choice but to return to their aunt's home. They are already thin and exhausted; they can't afford to starve for long.

Despite news that their cousin has been captured, the boys' aunt welcomes them back, but their relief is short-lived. It's not long before they're discovered. The dragoons surround the house and take the brothers prisoner. *Crash!* The frightening echo of splintering glass and dishes fills the air. *Snap!* Table legs are broken into pieces. The family watches in horror as the British soldiers destroy the house from top to bottom.

The demolition is complete.

An arrogant officer gives fourteen-year-old Andrew a command: "Polish my boots!"

The boy's fear and distress over his aunt's broken dishes dissolves into anger. He stands his ground and refuses to obey, and the officer draws his sword to strike him down. The courageous young rebel throws up his hand to protect himself, but the blade slices through it before cutting him deeply on the head.

Undaunted, blood trickling down his cheek, he stands tall and stubborn, daring the soldier to strike again.

Andrew Jackson does not surrender. He will not polish the enemy's boots. The future seventh president of the United States will carry scars from the gashing wounds of the Revolutionary War on his hand and head until the day he dies. Like those scars, defiance and courage will follow him all the days of his life.

Chapter One:
The Man With Handsome Eyes

President Andrew Jackson shaped history in a way that still influences the United States today some 250 years later. Colorful and controversial, he was different from the rich and well-educated presidents before him like George Washington and Thomas Jefferson.

☞ **Fast Fact:** President Jackson was the first president born in a log cabin.

President Jackson's poor immigrant parents taught him the value of religious freedom and hard work. Later, his service in the Revolutionary War drummed into him a passionate love for his new homeland and the importance of democracy.

Andrew Jackson, an Indian fighting military man, found himself the first president truly voted in by the voice of the people as the electoral process for America changed during his lifetime. He is credited with early American development that includes Tennessee, Louisiana, and Florida. His admirers remember him as a hero of the West. His critics remember him as a rebel with a terrible temper.

The seventh president, honored as a true man of the people, advanced the ideals of democracy throughout all of the branches of the government so the will of the people could be heard. When he left office, President Jackson passed on an organized and well-established new Democratic party.

Only a Mother

Andrew Jackson's parents, Andrew and Elizabeth Jackson, were Scotch-Irish immigrants who followed their brothers and sisters to America to find work and independence. They came from a region of Northern Ireland known as Ulster. This area was the northernmost province of the country and was populated with Scottish immigrants. The Scots had fled religious battles between James I of England and Roman Catholic clans in the 1600s.

The Scotch-Irish settled originally in Ireland's eastern part of Ulster and were mostly Presbyterians. Known for their courage, they brought with them a culture of battle and an appetite for adventure, but it was not war that drove them to America. Due to drought, a plant disease called rot, and terrible living standards, the Scotch-Irish, or Ulsters, as they came to be called, flocked to the American colonies with their sights set on Pennsylvania. Eventually, cheaper land opportunities tempted them to travel further south. Andrew and Elizabeth's families took part in this migration that spread beyond the borders of Pennsylvania.

The senior Andrew Jackson was the son of a linen draper, but he and his brothers chose agriculture as their livings, because England's taxation over Irish wool and other exports make life almost impossible to live in Ireland. After Andrew's brother fought the French and the Indians in America,

This hand-colored map, published in 1715, shows the Kingdom of Ireland. The main regions are Ulster, Connacht, Leinster, and Munster. Ulster is the region in light green on the upper right-hand side of the map. (Map courtesy of Library of Congress)

he returned and told Andrew and Elizabeth about how anyone could become a landowner in America. This was something that would never happen for their poor families in Ireland.

Elizabeth became convinced the idea was a good one. Four of her own sisters had good lives in America in a region called the Carolinas. It seemed like the perfect solution for a young couple, and their two young sons who needed a new and promising life. Their ancestors had left Scotland for Ireland, but found no freedom there. It seemed the right thing to do to continue the search for a home of peace and plenty. This meant traveling halfway around the world. The family left for America with two little boys, Hugh and Robert, in the spring of 1765. They arrived to find a lonely and sometimes forbidding land full of wild animals and savages.

No one is sure exactly which port the Jackson family sailed into, but it is assumed they stepped off their ship in America somewhere south of Philadelphia. They decided to head to a small, frontier settlement called Waxhaw, South Carolina, to join Elizabeth's sisters. It's possible they traveled down the Delaware River, but it's certain they found themselves on a long journey through undeveloped country with few places to rest. In order to reach the Carolinas and Waxhaw, they had to travel through Indian Territory. The family arrived safely and settled near one of Elizabeth's sisters named Jane Crawford.

Fast Fact: *The Catawba Indians in the area were peaceful and liked to trade with white settlers.*

The town of Waxhaw took its name from another Indian tribe that once roamed the area and were called the *Wysacky*. It was just a few miles from the North Carolina border, but the land Andrew Sr. claimed for his family was quite a long walk from town. Land was not cheap for immigrants who had spent everything they had to travel to America, so Andrew searched far and wide for unclaimed earth to make his own. He began working a piece of property in an area called Twelve Mile Creek.

It was hard work. Trees had to be cut and cleared. Soil had to be plowed. It must have seemed like life was finally working out for the new settlers when Elizabeth found herself expecting another baby, but fate had other plans. Andrew Sr. injured himself lifting a heavy log, and for some reason, he never recovered. He suddenly became ill and died. Right after this terrible tragedy, his third son was born fatherless in a dangerous and untamed country. Young Elizabeth now had three little children and no money.

"His Eyes Were Handsome"

Named in memory of his father, young Andrew Jackson grew up with his Uncle James, Aunt Jane, and their children in Waxhaw after his father's death. He always remembered Elizabeth as a loving mother who seemed to feel a need to work hard to earn them a place in the Crawford home. His birthday was March 15, 1767, and he claimed he was born in South Carolina at the Crawford's home.

 Fast Fact: *The Crawford house was on the North and South Carolina border. Today, both states still argue over Andrew Jackson's birth state.*

With a busy mother and aunt, Andrew found himself influenced as much by his young friends in Waxhaw as he was by other adults. Andrew had freckles, he was skinny, and he was as stubborn as molasses on a cold winter day, but he would fight for anything he felt worthwhile. One admiring rival from his boyhood days once said that Andrew would not turn down a fight. Even though he might be beaten or thrown to the ground several times in a wrestling match, he would always get back up. No one could make the Jackson boy stay down.

What did Andrew Jackson look like? As an older young man living in North Carolina to study law, his lanky body and freckled complexion didn't change much, but everyone makes a huge deal about his dazzling blue stare. He was still sharp, thin, and pointy. His complexion looked pallid and spotted. His hair color, a gift from his Scotch-Irish ancestry, glowed a very dark red.

When he wasn't defending his honor or someone else's, Andrew was thought to have a calm and gentle manner. He was not the most handsome or charming man in the room, but from his boyhood day and onward, the fiery, short-tempered redhead drew people — and trouble — toward him like bees to a hive.

Roosters and Horses

Elizabeth Jackson took care of Andrew and his cousins and helped manage the Crawford house. In keeping with their Ulster roots, she raised him in the Presbyterian religion. She recognized his intelligence in his early years and hoped he would be a minister. However, it wasn't too long before she knew the youngest of her boys had a strong will and awful temper.

Miss Annie Jarrett, a young woman of the time living near him in North Carolina recorded: "…his eyes were handsome. They were very large, a kind of steel blue, and when he talked to you, he always look straight into your own eyes" (Brands, 2005).
(Photo credit: Photospin.com)

Andrew's mother gave up on the idea of a preacher in the family pretty fast.

Ultimately, when Elizabeth's dreams of a preacher son were surrendered, Andrew was sent away to boarding school when he turned eleven. Under the eye of Dr. William Humphries, he learned his numbers and letters as well as some geography, Latin, and Greek. Unfortunately, other things captured Andrew's attention that must have seemed far more exciting than book learning.

One pastime he kept up with all his life was horses. They were an important part of existence in Colonial America, and young Andrew took right to them. He reportedly loved to race his horses against those of his friends.

Fast Fact: By the time Andrew was 16, he earned the right to be considered an authorized horse appraiser.

This gift of working with animals would later prove useful during the Revolutionary War. Afterward, raising thoroughbreds and horseracing on a grand scale would become a hobby that his foes would criticize him for, and it would ruin all of the good luck of an unexpected inheritance.

Besides being athletic and working with large animals, he loved to participate in cockfighting, too. This sport of pitting one rooster against another to watch them duel to the death was a fact of life during the time period and a very popular event. Young Andrew even went so far as to write a "memorandum" on how to do it.

Titled "A Memorandum How to Feed a Cock Before You Him Fight," he anonymously advises,

"Take and give him some Pickle Beaf Cut fine 3 times a Day and give him sweet Milk instead of water to Drink give him Dry Indien Corn that hase been Dryn Up in smoke givehim lighte wheat Bread Soken in sweet Milk feed him as Much as he can Eat for Eaight Days Orrange Town in Orange County"

—March the 22nd 79

In case you can't speak 18th century English, that basically translates to this:

"Take your rooster and feed him finely cut pickled beef for breakfast, lunch, and dinner. Serve him some sweet milk — no water. Give him that dry Indian corn that your mom uses to decorate the house for Thanksgiving, and throw in some wheat bread that has been soaking in some of the sweet milk. Feed him as much as humanly possible for about a week."

Andrew's avoidance of books and lack of opportunity for a formal education would haunt him when he became involved in politics as an adult. Unlike his presidential forerunners who were well schooled, the politician Andrew Jackson couldn't spell very well, and people made fun of him for it. Whether it was the lack of education or perhaps a condition known today as dyslexia, the orphan president couldn't spell at all, but he still wrote with power and influence. His supporters defended his weakness in grammar by pointing out all of his many lifelong adventures and experiences that, they claimed, gave him the advantage over his fancy competitors.

A Boy Goes to War

By the time young Andrew was ten-years-old, his country was at war for independence. England had passed the Stamp Act of 1765.

What's the Stamp Act? The Stamp Act created a tax on all types of paperwork, newspapers, almanacs, and just about anything else that could be printed — even playing cards and dice.

The American colonists rebelled because the Stamp Act had been declared without any representation in their behalf. The English Parliament repealed the tax the next year, but then it issued another law saying that Britain could tax its colonies wherever and whenever it desired. By then, it was too late. The Stamp Act had brought the colonists together and united them as one body. By 1776, after more taxes and problems, the young nation chose to fight for its freedom and rule itself.

The Revolutionary War was terrible. The experienced British Empire understood the best way to beat a nation in battle was to turn people against each other. In America, the South had many loyalists known as Tories, which would be a curse on the insurgent Jackson family. It became pretty clear that this war would make neighbors fight each other, and like all of Britain's wars, it would be bloody.

Elizabeth Jackson was a defiant rebel. With her now 13-year-old son, the family escaped British forces that reached Waxhaw and burned the colonists' barns and homes. Andrew was too young to fight, but the rebel army made use of him and his horsemanship as a scout and courier, someone who delivers packages and mail. His older brother, Hugh, was killed, and the news must have destroyed the family. Andrew became a soldier after that, and within a year, he experienced another horrible death. His cousin was shot while they were on guard duty and Andrew was standing right beside him. Young Andrew may have been next if it had not been for a fake bugle call in the forest nearby that made the enemy run, because they feared a rebel attack.

The war did not get any easier. In an unfortunate stroke of luck, a unit of British dragoons decided to search through Waxhaw for any hiding rebels. Andrew and his brother, Robert, hid in the woods for three days. Hungry, thirsty, and as one can imagine, exhausted beyond belief, the boys returned to their Aunt Jane's home for help. Her generosity cost her dearly when the dragoons captured them in the Crawford home at breakfast time. For punishment, they destroyed everything in the house, making the family and their cousins watch.

To further shame the rebel boys, one officer ordered Andrew to clean his boots, and Andrew flat out refused. It is said that he declared, "Sir, I am a prisoner of war, and claim to be honorably treated as such" (Donahoe's Magazine, 1892). Whether or not the officer really meant to kill him, the blade sliced Andrew's hand and then gashed his head. Despite what must have been hot, streaming blood, he stood tall and refused to obey the order. The officer did not swing at him again.

Again, his life was spared. The dragoons needed a scout to lead them to a wanted rebel's home. Having no choice but to obey, Andrew took them to the home of a rebel by the name of Thompson. Wisely, he chose the longer and more obvious of two routes, so that the man was able to see the British forces coming and could escape long before they arrived.

Having tricked the dragoons, he was now useless. Andrew, Robert, and their Uncle Crawford were official prisoners. The British marched them for miles to the town of Camden and a rebel prison camp without any medical attention or supplies. There they found no beds, clothing, or medicine for more than 200 prisoners. There was little to no food or water. Sick and dying men lay all around.

Before long, small pox, a terrible disease, spread through the camp like the plague. The dead rebels and friends of Andrew were left unburied. Somehow, in another miraculous stroke of luck, he didn't catch the disease while he was imprisoned. As a grown man, the thing he would remember most about being a British prisoner were the sounds of dying men.

The prison camp in Camden must have made it seem to the rebels like they were already dead. Andrew and Robert were divided up when it was discovered that they were brothers. Their shoes and jackets were taken away from them. The war dragged on, and the prisoners continued to starve or die from sickness and injuries. Andrew, however, had one last ace up his sleeve, and it saved him from death. That card was his passionate, brave mother who loved him more than life.

Elizabeth was just as determined a person as her son. When she heard of her children's imprisonment, she wasted no time traveling the forty miles from home to rescue them. She risked attacks by Indians and her own capture by the Tories if they discovered that she was not loyal to England. When she reached the Camden prison camp, she was able to convince the authorities to trade the boys for American prisoners, and the brothers were set free.

They set home with no food, shoes, or coats for the boys. They only had two horses between the three of them. Andrew walked. Robert caught smallpox. By the time they finally reached Waxhaw, Robert died within days, and Andrew became ill with the disease his sibling had brought home. His mother tended to him desperately.

Somehow, the future president's life was spared, and he survived the fever and rash that tormented his weak body. Just when he began to feel better, his mother left home again without him to find his cousins. She left Andrew alone and traveled 160 miles to Charleston where they were being held prisoners.

Elizabeth never returned. She died of cholera before she could finish her mission. The last thing her surviving son had of hers was a package of her clothes. Her influence on him, however, was never completely forgotten. Many admirers of Andrew Jackson believe the only thing of value he had when he found himself orphaned and alone was the guidance and memory of his invincible mother.

Before she left for Charleston, Elizabeth gave Andrew advice that he would remember all the days of his life. In her powerful message at his bedside she impressed upon him the importance of honesty, self-respect, loyalty, and forgiveness.

She told him:

"Andrew, if I should not see you again, I wish you to remember and treasure up some things I have already said to you: In this world you will have to make your own way. To do that you must have friends. You can make friends by being honest, and you can keep them by being steadfast. You must keep in mind that friends worth having will in the long run expect as much from you as they give to you. To forget an obligation or be ungrateful for a kindness is a base crime — not merely a fault or a sin, but an actual crime. Men guilty of it sooner or later must suffer the penalty. In personal conduct be always polite but never obsequious. No one will respect you more than you esteem yourself. Avoid quarrels as long as you can without yielding to imposition. But sustain your manhood always. Never bring a suit at law for assault and battery or for defamation. The law affords no remedy for such outrages that can satisfy the feelings of a true man. Never wound the feelings of others. Never brook wanton outrage upon your own feelings. If you ever have to vindicate your feelings or defend your honor, do it calmly. If angry at first, wait till your wrath cools before you proceed" (Buell, 1904).

Andrew finished recovering from smallpox while living with his Uncle James Crawford. Regarding his mother's death, he later admitted, "I felt utterly alone."

His mother's counsel to avoid quarrels did not stay in his memory for very long. During his short time with his extended family, he found himself involved in another dispute with an officer. This time, it was an American soldier who liked to talk and brag. Tired of hearing the man's exaggerations of his military service and tales of war action, the sarcastic teenager responded, "Probably all the killing he had ever done was beef-critters and sheep to feed the real fighting men of the army" (Buell, 1904).

The childhood days of Andrew Jackson were tragic and sad. He knew nothing but sadness in what should have been the best days of his life. The world as he knew it, robbed him of a father, home, freedom, happiness, and eventually, his mother and brothers. He was not an aristocrat and did not know what it was like to be rich or popular. It's no wonder this future politician would grow up to defend and support the Democratic party of the people.

(Photo courtesy of Library of Congress)

Chapter Two:
From Schoolroom to Courtroom

Andrew recovered from smallpox and decided it was time to leave his uncle's home. He had received only a limited amount of education in his mischievous youth. However, rather than returning to his studies, it may be around this time that he worked in a saddle maker's shop. He probably wasn't committed to this kind of task, because before he could decide on his lifelong career, he received news of an amazing inheritance. A large gift of money had been left to him by a grandparent still in Ireland.

Fast Fact: *The inheritance Andrew received, about $300, is estimated to have been today's equivalent of over $40,000.*

Life must have suddenly seemed full of epic possibilities. In order to claim his family fortune, Andrew learned he would have to travel to Charleston.

He didn't waste any time.

The war was rapidly coming to a close by the end of 1782. The British were eager to negotiate an end to the bloodshed since their surrender at Yorktown. Just as British forces began to leave the southern coastal city of Charleston, Andrew arrived with other rebels and colonists eager to take it back. It had been under British control since 1779 and was in rough shape, but it still offered many temptations to any young man with a lot of money. With sports, gaming, and plenty of taverns, Andrew discovered a whole new and exciting world. And he was rich.

Rather than invest the money his relative had left him, Andrew decided to indulge in his love of betting. He gambled on anything and everything — from sports to cards to dice. Sometimes he got lucky and it proved worthwhile.

> ☞ **Fast Fact:** Andrew's weakness for fine horses, which was a luxury at this time, caused him to get involved in a bet on his own horse that he won with a single roll of the dice.

The luck did not last long though. Within a matter of weeks, he was a broke 16-year-old with no family or prospects. He returned to Waxhaw where all he had to his name was his father's 200 acres of land.

Going home meant finding a job, working the family land, or going back to school. According to history, Andrew did return to his basic education and finish, but he must have felt too old or wise for further schooling, because his next whim was to offer himself up to a local country school as a teacher. Teaching may or may not have been his dream job; it certainly didn't pay well, and he wasn't respected as a great brain. He spent one term teaching and changed his mind again. Law, he decided, would be the best way to get the respect he wanted and make himself acceptable in society.

A Pathway to Law

Becoming a lawyer 200 years ago was not as difficult as it is today. The young men who wanted to practice law did not have to go to college, then survive years of law school, deal with stress, major competition, or starve because of the high cost of tuition. Consider Abraham Lincoln, who was born in a log cabin in Illinois yet destined to be president. All Lincoln was required to do by the state of Illinois was prove he was a man of moral character. According to the law, he only needed to present a court certificate from any county in the state that said he was a good man. Things weren't that much different earlier in 1787.

Law in the 18th century was a proper career. It didn't require an aristocratic bloodline, and outside of the "modern" cities, passing the examination was not difficult on the frontier. It was the perfect way for a young man with only a little money and a few connections to get ahead. Now recognized by England as an independent country, things were changing in America, and Andrew embraced the excited attitudes and ambitions of the colonists who were now free to govern themselves.

Not far from Waxhaw, in Salisbury, North Carolina, Andrew approached a lawyer about an apprenticeship to learn the practice. The lawyer, known as Spruce Macay, agreed. He had other apprentices in his business, one a man named John McNairy. McNairy would prove to be an important part of Andrew's future. Together and by day, the interns took care of paperwork, ran errands, and learned the craft as best they could. The truth was that Lawyer Macay was a frontier attorney who didn't have much to offer two ambitious young men.

After hours, their personal business was a different matter. Andrew soon picked up a bad reputation for partying, gambling, and getting involved in all kinds of trouble at night. Apparently, this didn't bother Macay. The mentor kept him on. Andrew stayed with him for two years before transferring his studies to an unusual character known as Colonel Stokes.

Colonel John Stokes, a Revolutionary War veteran, must have understood Andrew. In return, the young lawyer in training must have admired the old man back. Stokes was popular for using a silver nob as an attachment on his amputated hand and pounding it for effect in court. Even if he didn't shock everyone by looking like a pirate, he must have certainly had a big personality. In a 1790 letter to George Washington from the House of Representatives John Steele, Stokes was well recommended for a position of district judge in North Carolina.

John Steele's signature
(Photo courtesy of Library of Congress)

Of this Colonel who trained Andrew, Steele wrote in his letter:
"This Gentleman is a native of Virginia, descended from a
very respectable family, was a captain in the Sixth Regiment
of that state in the late War, continued in service untill
Colo. Beaufort was defeated in So. Carolina, when unfortu-
nately he lost (amon[gst] other wounds) his right hand.
He then setled in No. Carolina, has practiced the law
ever since, with reputation, and success, has been frequently
a member of the State legislature wherein he supported
a very respectable, and honorable rank, both as a man
of business, and a man of abilities, was a member of the
Convention and very instrumental in bringing about
the ratification of the Constitution, is at this time Colo.
Commandt of a Regt of militia Cavalry, and additional
Judge of the supreme Court of Law and Equity in that State.
Notwithstanding the loss of his right hand, few men write
better than he does with the other, and is extreemely capable
of business" (Steele, 1790).

The intelligent Andrew Jackson made a smart move moving over to the office of the well-respected and experienced Colonel with the silver nob. In less than a year of training under Colonel Stokes, he took his examination before the North Carolina Superior Court of Law and Equity and passed. Ironically, none of his wild ways were brought up during the test. In fact, the board stated that Andrew was a candidate who had been recommended with "unblemished moral character" (Brands, 2005). It was 1787. Andrew was only 20 years old.

Boys Behaving Badly

Whether it was his poor education, his bad temper, or the political choices he made, Andrew Jackson was a controversial president not only while he was alive but even today. When he died, the writer of his eulogy said of him, "It can hardly be expected that the present generation will do justice to the character of Jackson, for his opponents have ever been most bitter enemies, and his friends almost his worshippers" (Sellers, 1958).

From his childhood days in Waxhaw and onward, he always seemed to find himself with a terrible reputation. He scraped by in school; gambled at cards, cock fighting, and horseracing; swore; and brawled. While in Salisbury training to be a lawyer, he was quickly known as a man of mischief. With the other law apprentices, he played cards, bet on animals, and pulled off practical jokes that were shady and rude.

> **Fast Fact:** In one famous story, Andrew invited two women with bad reputations to a Christmas ball, much to the horror and embarrassment of everyone there. The joke went over so badly he tried to excuse himself by saying he didn't really think they'd have the nerve to show up.

Nothing changed afterward. The bad behavior continued. After one night out with his friends, the party threw glasses into a fire. This didn't seem exciting enough, so the men, including Andrew, burned the furniture and drapes. Most of the people of Salisbury later said they never thought he would live for very long much less become President. The women didn't want him brought to their homes, and the young ladies were sure he was "by no means a Christian man" (Brands, 2005).

Lawyer for Hire

Things for Andrew didn't improve the moment he was admitted by North Carolina to practice law. Within two months, he found himself charged with destruction and trespassing. Apparently he thought it still okay to keep partying, damage property, and not pay his bills. Luckily, he was able to settle the charges out of court and was not disbarred, or expelled, before his career had even begun.

Andrew quickly found there was not a lot of work for a young, new lawyer on the North Carolina frontier. He often had to travel for miles around to find business. In Randolph County in 1788, he charged a man named Samuel Graves, for illegally seizing and selling someone's mare and saddle. Another job in Surrey County meant defending someone for stealing, but the case was lost, and Andrew didn't get paid. By all accounts, his next address was in Martinsville, North Carolina. There wasn't a great deal for a lawyer to do in this town either, so acting as the constable was the next best thing. Two of his friends owned a general store there, and it's likely that he helped them out off and on to make extra cash.

Even on a tight budget, Andrew still found time to socialize during those lean years.

What was Andrew Jackson really like? One young woman recalled of Andrew, "He always dressed neat and tidy and carried himself as if he was a rich man's son" (Brands, 2005).

His important connections still counted, too. A growing settlement first established by a Virginia family along the western Cumberland River needed a judge. Andrew's old friend John McNairy got the job, but he asked Andrew to come along to the capital of this region called the Mero district and fill in as a solicitor, which is a fancy word for lawyer.

A Road to Tennessee

Nashville was the capital of the Mero District and it was a part of North Carolina in 1788. Settled by a Virginia man by the name of John Donelson ten years earlier, it would become a part of the state of Tennessee years later. Nashville was hundreds of miles away. Andrew and McNairy found themselves traveling through Indian and animal-infested land just to get as far as the city of Jonesboro. There, he took a civil case that pitted him against another lawyer who had turned Andrew down for an apprenticeship. The fiery, easily offended Andrew took some of his opponent's remarks in court too personal, and he challenged the man to a fight. The offending lawyer was incredulous. Andrew wanted to duel.

McNairy and his hotheaded prosecutor made it to Nashville with sixty other families in their party in October of 1788. Again, there were Indians, and on this journey, a tragic attack left some dead. It's possible that Andrew might have been killed, too, but he wandered off to investigate a strange owl call that sounded suspicious. The Indians attacked while was he was gone. Just as in the Revolution, astonishing circumstances spared his life that night.

When they arrived in Nashville, it probably felt like civilization to the tired travelers. The white settlers in the area still had problems with

Indians, and the country teemed with other predators — bear, bobcats, coyotes, and even snakes. As for the thousands of settlers Andrew would have to deal with, many of them had fled the Revolutionary War and had no respect for law. This meant plenty of work and lots of debtors to throw in jail. Andrew would be busy, and busy meant money.

> ☞ **Fast Fact:** Black bears in Tennessee are black in color, but can be brown or cinnamon colors in other places. They can grow six feet long and be as tall as three feet high up to the shoulders. That's a big animal to deal with if it's angry or hungry!

There were lawsuits of all kinds with all of the debt collectors there. Andrew soon found himself popular and successful. This meant he could think about opening his own law practice. He had lots of support from all of his satisfied customers, and they weren't just creditors. He made friends with landowners, too.

First Lady Rachel Jackson
(Photo courtesy of Library of Congress)

Chapter Three:
The Lovely Rachel Donelson

Nashville, or the early Cumberland area, was settled by the prominent Colonel John Donelson, and he had a daughter. Rachel Donelson was born probably about June of 1767, in the state of Virginia. Her father was a member of the House of Burgesses. Her mother was Rachel Stockley. It's believed Rachel, the future Mrs. Andrew Jackson, was born near present day Chatham, Virginia, the tenth of eleven children. Her family was respectable enough to provide the opportunity for her to be introduced to famous American leaders like George Washington and Thomas Jefferson.

Fast Fact: According to the National First Ladies Library, Rachel not only visited former presidents at their homes, but she was also acquainted with the infamous Patrick Henry — you know, the "Give me liberty, or give me death!" guy.

The Donelson family was fearless and was prepared to open up the West to get wealthy. A planter and slave owner, Colonel Donelson took his family to settle the early Nashville area on the Cumberland River when Rachel was 13 years old. The young teenager, with only a basic education, traveled over 1,000 miles through dangerous Indian lands. Quite a scary adventure for a young lady! Their arrival, after a time, didn't quite go as planned. The family retreated to Kentucky for safety from the Indians, and it was there that Rachel, now 17, met a man named Captain Lewis Robards. She married the army officer and was left behind when her family returned once again to the Cumberland area.

Things didn't go so well for the Donelson family after returning without their daughter. Indians had been the main reason to leave, and they were still a problem when the family returned. Worse, there were now thieves and robbers, too. One heartbreaking day, Rachel's father, Colonel Donelson, did not return from his job surveying land for new settlers. His body was found in the woods, and both Indians and robbing highwaymen were blamed. No one was ever sure who killed him, but he was not missing his scalp — only his wallet.

Married life for Rachel as Mrs. Robards wasn't so wonderful either. When her father died, Rachel still lived in Kentucky with her husband and mother-in-law who took in boarders, or renters. Her husband, Robards, is described as being mean and jealous. Anyone who paid her special attention created problems, and one of those was a man known as Peyton Short. He was a boarder of Rachel's mother-in-law, and he and Rachel must have gotten along. They were too friendly for Rachel's husband. Robards believed she had betrayed him, and he threw her out of the house.

Rachel must have been relieved. The couple tried to work things out for a time, but by 1790, she decided to leave him for good. She asked a lawyer living in her mother's house for help. His name was Andrew Jackson. Like her, Andrew was a devout Presbyterian. Rachel spent some time with relatives in Mississippi, and that same year her husband asked the state of Kentucky for a divorce. Robards claimed Rachel had abandoned him.

Quite the Beauty

Rachel was friendly and vivacious, and later in life is recorded as being capable of running a plantation while her husband was gone. She was also known as a charming hostess. Her guests and her husband respected and adored her.

> **What did Rachel Donelson look like?** In her youth, Rachel Donelson's dark hair and dark eyes won her many admirers. Stories say she had a lovely full figure with shining brunette hair. Besides "full red lips," she had a sweet expression with "rippling smiles and dimples." Paintings today show a modest, pretty woman with serious eyes and plump cheeks.

Not everyone thought she was wonderful, though. Many people who were more educated and fashionable found her to be too country for their liking. She seemed to prefer her own family, poetry, and her Bible over parties and other social activities. Surely in her own way she must have been an introvert. When President Andrew Jackson later won the White House, it is said she remarked she'd "rather be a door-keeper in the house of God than to live in that palace in Washington" (Britannica).

Rachel had her own funny habits. As if her lack of education and sophistication weren't enough, she was also known to smoke a corncob pipe. Her friends and family defended her saying it was a solution recommended by her doctors for shortness of breath. This smoking habit was made fun of by all of the couple's enemies who loved to criticize the politician's choice of a wife. The media then was just as cruel as it can be today, too. One compared her to a "fat dumpling" (Brands, 2005). No wonder she didn't want to go to Washington!

Courtship and Marriage

During the time Rachel was back home in Nashville living with her widowed mother in their boarding house, Lewis Robards did come back and try to get her to come home to Kentucky. He came and went a couple of times, but Rachel had already made up her mind not to be a poorly treated wife. History suspects that it was after Robards left the second time that Andrew began to really care about her.

About this time, Andrew was a boarder of Mrs. Donelson. He may not have lived in the very same house, but in lodgings on the property. One day, news came that Lewis Robards planned to return again, and Andrew helped Mrs. Donelson and the frightened Rachel escape to Natchez, Mississippi to live with relatives. The year was 1791, and it was then that Andrew and Rachel heard about Robards' petition for divorce.

Andrew returned home after helping the Donelson's escape, and Robards was in town. News came that Robards was telling everyone he had gotten his divorce, and Andrew believed it. Those that later defended Andrew and Rachel said that Robards lied on purpose. He wanted Andrew and Rachel to marry so he could ruin them both when it was found out Rachel was still married to another man.

They married, according to some rumors, in Natchez, Mississippi, that year of 1791. Some believe they did not marry until three years later in Nashville. Either way, Robards did not get the divorce until September of 1793. The confusion over the paperwork later destroyed Rachel's reputation and was used against her when Jackson began to move up in politics.

(Photo courtesy of Library of Congress)

Hearing from both sides of the story:

Lewis Robards claimed Rachel was a flirt and had left Kentucky by her own choice. He always believed Jackson had seduced her away from him, and that's why he was never able to win Rachel back.

Jackson, Rachel, and their families never stopped accusing Robards of being cruel and violent. According to their side of the story, Rachel fled to Mississippi because she thought she might be killed.

Defending Rachel's reputation kept Jackson busy. He would stand up to anyone who gossiped or said awful things about his wife.

Fast Fact: In 1806, Andrew Jackson challenged Charles Dickinson to duel to the death for insulting his wife, Rachel. Jackson won.

During the elections when Jackson ran for president years later, his political enemies spread the story that he had stolen Rachel from her first husband and run away with her to Mississippi. The Spanish owned what was then Mississippi and only recognized Catholic marriages. Jackson's enemies used this fact to encourage the newspapers to spread insulting stories about Rachel and her mother. They called them terrible names. Even though Jackson remarried Rachel in Nashville because his friends and advisors insisted on it just in case, some people never accepted or forgave them.

It didn't matter to Jackson what people thought of him, but he always believed in his darling Rachel. He was very protective of her and was known to be perfectly devoted to her in every way. Maybe it was because he had lost all of his family, and she was all that he had. They were never able to have children of their own, but fate allowed them to be loving parents.

In 1809, Jackson and Rachel had been married for fifteen years. They must have wished desperately for children, because when Rachel's brother became the father of twins, the family needed helped raising two babies. Rachel and her sister-in-law came to an agreement that the Jacksons would raise one of the twin boys as their own. Jackson and Rachel's brother agreed, too, and the twin baby boy was named Andrew Jackson Junior.

Jackson made sure the baby was quickly and legally adopted. Friends and family watched the new parents give their new son everything they had never had.

Fast Fact: Andrew Jackson Junior was so loved that one story tells of a time a friend visited the Jackson home to find a lamb inside. Andrew explained that his little boy had worried the little lamb would be too cold outdoors, and so the animal was rescued and brought in at once.

Later, Jackson and his wife agreed to raise two other nephews. They raised John and Andrew Donelson Jackson after their father died. Another boy, Andrew Hutchings, became their ward in 1819. Obviously, no matter what some people in society thought about the Jacksons, their families loved and trusted them enough to help raise their children.

The lovely Rachel Donelson died of a heart attack unexpectedly after Jackson won his first presidential election in December of 1828. She had been stressed during the election, and the rude stories printed about her past in the papers didn't help. Jackson had her body dressed in in the gown she had planned to wear on his first special day in Washington and buried her on the property of their family home, known as the Hermitage.

All kinds of people came from all over the country to Rachel's funeral. There were around 10,000 people of every color and from every social class. Jackson's good friend Sam Houston, who was now governor of Tennessee, helped carry Rachel to her final resting place.

"

Even though his heart was destroyed, Jackson found the courage to speak during the service.

"I am now President of the United States and in a short time must take my way to the metropolis of my country; and, if it had been God's will, I would have been grateful for the privilege of taking her to my post of honor and seating her by my side; but Providence knew what was best for her" (**http://firstladies.org**).

Years later, he wrote a letter to Rachel's nephew, Samuel Hays. In it, he asked about Rachel's grave and made it clear how much he still loved and missed her:

"You will oblige me by giving me a full description of all my mares & colts & their looks & vallue-and my Dr Saml give a faithful description of the garden, the tomb of my dear wife, & whether the roses & flowers, which I directed to be planted around it, has been so planted, & whether the row of flowers between the House & front gate is attended to- Say to old Hannah & Betty that all those that were planted by the instructions of your dear aunt, I wish carefully cultivated & preserved, until I return That garden is now to me a consecrated spot, & I wish it carefully attended to, particularly the square around the sacred Tomb" (Register of Kentucky State Historical Society, 1943).

Chapter Four: Politics and Dueling

In 1791, after Jackson took Rachel and her mother to Mississippi to get away from Lewis Robards, he returned to Nashville and went back to work as a prosecutor. Things had changed in the United States. Nashville was no longer a part of North Carolina; in 1787, it was given new boundaries in what the government called the Southwest Territory. This meant there was money to be made, not just as a lawyer, but as a land speculator and merchant storeowner, too. Jackson also built a stable and raced his horses.

Land speculating meant buying land. A speculator in Nashville would buy up available acres of good forest and farmland and wait for settlers to come in looking for land to buy. The speculator would hope that good land would be harder to find so he could sell his investment at a higher price. Jackson bought land that cost less than ten cents an acre and would resell it to settlers for up to three dollars.

Fast Fact: *If you adjust for inflation, it would be like someone purchasing land for just over $1 an acre and reselling it for around $45 an acre.*

This image shows a distant view of the Hermitage.
(Image courtesy of Library of Congress)

It seemed like a good idea. He went into business with a friend, and at one point owned tens of thousands of acres.

Because so much of his investment was still officially dangerous Indian Territory that was not really up for grabs, Jackson didn't make as much money with his business partner as he hoped in the long run. He traveled to Philadelphia to buy supplies for his store and to sell the land. He found a Mr. Allison to do business with, but made the mistake of using his land to pay for supplies for his store. This situation eventually landed him in terrible debt. Mr. Allison was also affected. Buying the land put him in debt, and he went to prison and later died there. In order to escape, Jackson had to sell his store located at Clover Bottom, Tennessee, and all of the stock. It paid the credit in Philadelphia, and probably saved his life.

Land speculating, it was clear, could be risky business. However, the business did give Jackson the opportunity to buy good real estate for himself. He and Rachel lived with Mrs. Donelson until he bought a plantation called Hunter's Hill in 1796. Eight years later, Rachel picked out a 425-acre property near the Cumberland River. They named it the Hermitage.

The Hermitage is a popular visitor's location in Nashville today. Built in the Greek Revival style, it took years to build with the main rooms completed between 1818 and 1819. The two-story brick mansion had a center hall with a parlor, dining room, and bedrooms on the ground floor. The upper floor had more bedrooms.

Fast Fact: *The Greek Revival style was the most popular type of architecture during the mid-1800s. It was popular because it was symbolic of tradition and democracy.*

Until it was ready, Jackson and Rachel lived in log buildings. They were slave owners and farmed cotton on the land, which was convenient to ship out with the river nearby. When Jackson was away, Rachel ran the plantation on her own, always waiting patiently for him to return home. During their years at the Hermitage, they hosted popular parties and welcomed famous guests. Many politicians visited them there including several famous figures like the vice president, Aaron Burr, and President James Monroe.

A Word on Slavery

In 1808, it became illegal to import slaves in the United States. This did not matter very much, because there were so many slaves already here, and they were having babies. In fact, the new law made slaveholders even wealthier, because the price of slaves went up. The enslaved people, called "servants" by their owners (maybe to ease their guilty consciences), were still treated with barbaric cruelty. They were lashed and tortured for punishment, especially when they tried to escape, and children were sold away from their mothers. By 1820, owning slaves in some parts of the country was frowned upon, but not enough.

> 👉 **Fast Fact:** By the year 1800, slaves counted as more than 17 percent of the country's population.

Raised in such poverty, Jackson and Rachel did not grow up with slaves working for their families. In 1788, this changed when a customer paid Jackson with a slave in place of money. The enslaved woman's name was Nancy. Rachel soon "inherited" two more enslaved people when her father died. According to the history of the Hermitage, there were only two slaves brought to the property when the Jacksons bought the land. Today, it's known that the house and the rest of the buildings were built by the hands of slaves who numbered at least over 100 before Jackson no longer bought or sold them.

Curiously, even with the large number of enslaved people listed among his holdings, Jackson was never considered to be a slave trader, but a slave owner. He took care of their physical needs and health and would not separate mothers and young children. However, he was reputed to be "brutal" when punishing, and it's certain that he did lash one slave who tried to escape. Jackson later tried to distance himself from the fact that he was involved in slavery during his presidential elections. By that time, slavery and politics did not go well together.

Today, archeologists surveying the slave's quarters at the Hermitage have found evidence of how the enslaved people there lived. Besides more cabins, they have dug up gun parts that may have been allowed for hunting. Animal bones, seeds, and charcoal show evidence of being self-sufficient. There are even signs of personal gardens. Glasses, slates for writing, pencils, beads, and marbles have also been found.

Politics

Even as a lawyer, Jackson was quite interested in society and politics. He only knew a little about the ins and out of being a politician, though. One of his first experiences paired him with a French merchant by the name of Anthony Fagot who wanted to increase trade in the territories. Jackson didn't know it, but his acquaintance was secretly working with the Spanish to win the primitive Cumberland area for Spain. Fagot went as far as naming the early Nashville area, Mero, after the Spanish Governor Míro, but his efforts were in vain. When Jackson realized what Fagot was up to, they were through. This taste of playing traitor may have influenced Jackson early on to consider the power of politics and military men, even if it only renewed his devotion to his country.

Politics came calling around the time he became a married man. Overseas, the French Revolution was raging, and Americans weren't all on the same side. The revolution in France was different than the war between the American colonists and Great Britain.

Fast Fact: The French Revolution was a civil war between the ruling aristocrats, the very poor peasants, and lower classes in Paris.

Americans like Thomas Jefferson who felt like less government worked best supported the lower class in the French revolt. Others felt that human nature was not to be trusted and that more government was needed in the lives of every citizen. Thomas Jefferson's supporters were named Republicans. Those who wanted more government control were called Federalists.

Jackson sympathized with the Republicans. He saw the divide in politics happening in the country when he visited Philadelphia to sell his land. When the new Southwest Territory was named with Nashville in the middle of it, it became clear to the people there that they would need a constitution. Jackson was a lawyer, and lawyers were rare on the frontier. He stepped forward, because he felt it was his duty to attend a Knoxville convention in January of 1796 as Nashville's delegate. Being the opinionated and determined man he was, he made his influence there felt by everyone else.

During the Knoxville convention, it was decided that the new constitution should be patterned just like the national government. While Jackson did not stand and give mad and fiery speeches, historical accounts show he was very clever. This delegate from Nashville would find someone who agreed with him on specific problems and have him stand and make a motion. This meant presenting an idea to put forward for a vote. Jackson would second the motion, which was necessary and needed. That way, he always got his agenda put before the rest of the delegates. He must have impressed a great deal of people during the convention, because later, after Tennessee was accepted to the Union, he was chosen as congressman.

Being a U.S. congressman meant Jackson had to travel back to Philadelphia. He avoided being chosen for the senate because of his young age, and besides, he didn't want it. Philadelphia was not exciting to him, and it was far away from his wife and home. Jackson was also different from the other politicians back East. He was not aristocratic and did not carry himself or speak the same way.

Fast Fact: *While a member of the House, President Jackson only made two speeches.*

He was also one of a very few who spoke out against George Washington's career as president. Jackson felt Washington's decisions on Indian matters and relationships with foreign countries went against what America had fought for in the Revolution. He was not impressed by Washington's departing speech. He thought it sounded too much like a king.

In one of his most pivotal acts as congressman for Tennessee, Jackson won money for an Indian fighter from Knoxville named John Sevier. The Tennessee militia and John Sevier had serious Indian trouble from the Cherokees. Men, women, and children who felt they lived lives as peaceful Americans were murdered by the Cherokee who saw their own lands shrinking because of the numerous white men. In 1793, after an attack on Knoxville by an army of 1200 Indians, the militia planned a battle to drive them back. It cost a great deal of money for the poor frontiersmen. Sevier now wanted payback for his men. The War Department denied them the money.

Jackson stood before the House and reminded the government that the men had sacrificed working their farms and the safety of their families to defend government land.

Fast Fact: *The Tennessee Militia was awarded $22,816 thanks to Andrew Jackson. Today, that would be around $400,000.*

John Sevier may have been thankful for his Tennessee congressman then, but they would later become violent enemies.

The congressman Andrew Jackson did not want to be reelected. He traveled home to Rachel and the Hermitage in the spring of 1797. His time off didn't last long, though. By the end of the year, he found himself elected to the Senate. He was old enough and well-respected in Tennessee now, but it wasn't the job he really wanted.

The Knoxville Indian fighter, John Sevier, was named as Brigadier General of the Tennessee Militia. Jackson had really tried for that title. When hiring his local commanders, Sevier passed up Jackson for a post and chose a personal friend instead. Jackson was offended, and when word got back to him, Sevier criticized him by calling him a "pitiful petty fogging lawyer" (Brands, 2005). Jackson immediately wrote him and challenged him to a duel. The older and more powerful man, Sevier, refused and wrote back a somewhat weak explanation for his words, which Jackson accepted as an apology. The hotheaded lawyer let him off with a notice. "I feel the … necessity of protecting my feelings and reputation whenever they are maliciously injured," Jackson wrote back in friendly warning.

He was a senator for the year 1798 and quickly returned home. Although he did nothing to wreak havoc in the Senate, his presence made it clear he was willing to step forward where he was needed, but not as a Federalist. He resigned from the Senate once he got home, but politics did not go away. Not long after he turned back to land dealing and agriculture, a letter from John Sevier offered up a big surprise. There was a position for a Tennessee State Supreme Court Judge, and Jackson had been recommended. It was too high and respectable a position for the former North

Carolina orphan to refuse. Hot temper, opinions, and all, Jackson accepted the judgeship and maintained the job for six years.

The Honorable Judge Jackson had no patience with dishonorable men. During his time as judge, he had accusers arrested for contempt of court, offered to meet them for duels, and assaulted them in the streets during breaks from the courtroom. In one instance, he again challenged John Sevier, who was now governor, at an assembly meeting in Knoxville. During a hot conversation, Sevier declared his enemies were "cowards and dare not meet him," and Jackson stepped forward and demanded an explanation. When the governor's son picked up a rock in defense of his father, the curse words flew.

Jackson invited Governor Sevier to meet him in a grove of trees to duel, but the infuriated politician dared him to meet up in the street in front of the entire public. Though recovering from an illness, Jackson showed up with a sword cane and challenged the governor who had brought a cutlass. They exchanged slurs and threats, and when the governor re-issued the challenge, a Colonel Martin grabbed Jackson by the arm and directed him safely back to their hotel, swearing and cursing all the way — if that is what is meant by witnesses who described them exchanging "insulting and abusive expressions" (Brands, 2005).

In another story, one defendant gave up his weapon when he met Judge Jackson in the street. It is rumored the rowdy drunk explained, "I looked him in the eye, and I saw shoot ... so I said to myself, says I: Hoss, it's about time to sing small, and so I did" (Brands, 2005).

Andrew Jackson was just as intimidating and fearless a judge as he was as a boy soldier. Everyone around him, from Nashville to Philadelphia, began to take notice. In 1802, the post for commander of the Tennessee Militia became available again. It was higher pay and something Jackson had his eye on before. John Sevier was no longer governor, and he wanted the post, too.

During an election the two men tied, and Sevier demanded a second vote. Jackson refused because it was not the law. He insisted the new governor decide, and on April 1, 1802, Andrew Jackson became Major General of the militia of his home state. The governor, Archibald Roane, was an old lawyer friend of Jackson's from North Carolina. Law had finally paid off.

About Those Famous Duels

Dueling in the 18th century was considered an acceptable way to resolve differences, especially if someone had been insulted enough to suffer damage to his or her reputation. Jackson was known to be sensitive to criticism and would defend himself or his Rachel to the death without any hesitation.

 Fast Fact: It was acceptable to just meet for a duel. Pistols could be fired in the air, and both contestants could walk away satisfied that they were brave enough to show up in the first place. This seemed to happen a great deal more than actual shootouts.

Another good way to avoid getting shot to death over a silly argument was to have a "second." A second would duel if for any reason his friend could not. Most of the time, it seems they really acted as peacemakers and tried to talk sense into everyone else.

Jackson was no stranger to the notion of a duel. Some historians believe he issued hundreds of challenges to fight. He delivered his first recorded challenge as a boy to the American solider boasting and bragging in his uncle's home. When Jackson called him out for exaggerating, and the captain threatened to have him horsewhipped, the teenager promised him if he tried, he would "send him to the other world."

The first official invitation ever issued by the future president is considered to have been for Mr. Waightstill Avery, the lawyer in Jonesboro who offended him during the civil suit before Jackson reached the Mero District. The challenge was slipped into an old book and presented to Avery, but he ignored it. Jackson had to re-issue the request the next day. Someone must have talked sense into Jackson, because in this first instance, he agreed to fire off pistols in the air and walk away.

It is only natural to believe Jackson would challenge Lewis Robards to a duel. The first husband of Rachel Jackson met with Jackson when the young lawyer approached him to defend his honor. He had not tried to steal Rachel away, and he hadn't done anything wrong. Robards did not believe him and threatened to beat him up. Jackson issued a challenge to duel, but Robards refused. It is said that Robards cursed and swore at him, then quickly retreated back to Kentucky without Rachel by his side.

The next major duel known is the nearly violent clash between Jackson and Governor John Sevier in Knoxville. The initial duel where both had agreed to step away and fire into the air had been fueled by Sevier's insults about Rachel. According to some historical accounts, this wasn't the end of it.

 Fast Fact: *Dueling wasn't legal in Tennessee, so Andrew Jackson agreed to meet John Sevier in nearby Virginia.*

Another duel was planned. Defenders of Jackson say he arrived first and then left when Sevier didn't show up. Defenders of Sevier say he was running late. Either way, they met along the way when Jackson was leaving and went right back to arguing and insulting one another. Sevier's horse reportedly ran away with his guns, and Jackson chased him behind a tree to shoot him, but his second talked him down.

The feuding between Jackson and Sevier never really ended. The men used friends and the newspapers to criticize each other and make insults. The bad press didn't hurt Jackson. He was the commander of the state's militia now, and the hostility supported his tough image of a man of honor who would defend his principles to the death. Their raging differences and disputes would affect the course of Tennessee politics for years to come.

Andrew Jackson's most deadly feud occurred in the early summer of 1806. It all began over horseracing, still one of his favorite past times. He had two good horses, Truxton and Greyhound, and he welcomed a challenge from any other horse owner.

A Mr. Joseph Erwin took him up on the bet. The wager was to be $2,000, but Erwin backed out. Whether he didn't think he could win or couldn't afford to lose, he changed his mind. Rumors began spinning that Jackson had called him names. Other people got involved, including Erwin's son-in-law, Charles Dickinson.

After a few months of insults and criticism between Jackson and Dickinson, a duel was the only way to settle it, and they decided to have it in Kentucky. Other critics were ignored, but Dickinson's challenging name of "coward" for Jackson made a fight unavoidable. Both men showed up. Each fired — Dickinson first — and then calmly, though wounded, Jackson fired back.

Dickinson was shot in the stomach. He never knew he'd hit Jackson, because the older politician didn't flinch.

After Dickinson crumpled to the ground, witnesses realized his opponent was shot only an inch from his heart. His jacket had disguised the blood, and he hadn't shown any pain. Unfortunately, the young Dickinson died shortly afterward. When Jackson returned home, critics in Nashville shamed him for what he had done, and many accused him of actually enjoying bloodshed.

There were others throughout the course of the future president's life that offered to exchange shots on the killing grounds. During the dispute between Jackson and Charles Dickinson, another friend of the crowd demanded satisfaction. His name was Nathaniel McNairy. Whether he was truly offended for his friends or wanted attention, he challenged Jackson to meet him in a duel. The event never happened because their seconds met first, and differences were settled without violence.

Jackson never managed to put dueling behind him without avoiding permanent injury. In the most personally dangerous of all of his gunfights, he took a bullet in the shoulder that caused him to nearly bleed to death at the Nashville Inn. The reason for the conflict happened earlier in 1813 when he'd acted as second for one of his men, William Carroll. Carroll was to fight the brother of one of Jackson's other military men. The brother's family felt furious over how the duel was conducted, and they declared war on the Jacksons.

It wasn't long before a chance meeting downtown turned deadly. The supporters of both men became entangled in whips and pistols after insults created a confrontation that went from gunfire to knives. No one was killed, but Jackson took the worst of it. Shot in his left shoulder and arm, he nearly bled out from a severed artery. Doctors wanted to amputate his arm, but he flat out refused.

Risking infection and death, he kept the bullet and his limb.

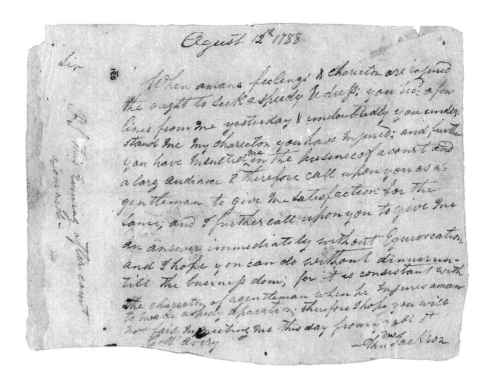

Andrew Jackson to Waightsell Avery, August 12, 1788
"(...) My charector you have injured; and further you have Insulted me
in the presence of a court and a larg audiance. I therefore call upon you as
a gentleman to give me satisfaction for the Same (...)"
(Image courtesy of Library of Congress)

Chapter Five: Indian War

Life in early Tennessee history meant risk and danger. Even before the Jacksons arrived, settlers dealt with the threat of Indian attacks on a daily basis. It's estimated that Indians killed a white person about every 10 days (Brands, 2005). This included women and children. The Indians in the area would attack within yards of public roads, burn farms, and plunder homes. They were as savage as the British, skinning entire heads and collecting scalps.

The raiding tribes were Cherokee. One chief said, "We cannot live without war" (Brands, 2005). Although they made treaties and traded for guns when they felt like it, the Cherokee hated the white settlers on their lands. During the Revolutionary War, they joined the British side like so many other Indian nations. This happened often, because they believed the British would hold back the multiplying numbers of white men.

> **Fast Fact:** The Cherokee were the native people of eastern Tennessee and western North Carolina. They ruled the Appalachian Mountains and believed in the ideas and lifestyles of war. A boy could only become a respected man by killing or capturing prisoners.

As Nashville grew and tried to push the Indians westward, a greater war brewed further south. There, the Creek Indians welcomed the great Shawnee leader, Tecumseh, from the North, and they embraced his visionary call to wage war against all whites.

The Red Sticks

The Creek Indians lived further south than their Cherokee neighbors. Today, their lands cover the regions of Georgia and Alabama. They farmed corn, beans, and squash. Wearing deerskin leggings and loose shirts, they fished and hunted for turkey and deer.

What did the Creek Indians look like? Their hair was worn long, and sometimes, they plucked their scalps on the sides, leaving only one long strip of hair worn down the center of the head. They tattooed and painted their bodies. They wore jewelry, too, usually made from deer antlers or boar tusks.

Like their Cherokee neighbors, and unlike Europeans, it mattered more to the Creeks what you accomplished in life than who your relatives might be.

The Creeks' first encounter with Europeans happened in the late 1530s, when Spanish explorer Hernando DeSoto came looking for gold. They did not have guns, but they did have spears, bows, tomahawks, and clubs. As white settlers moved in and prospered after the Revolutionary War, the tribes in the Creek Nation found themselves split on how to deal with the situation. Some Creeks, known as Lower Creeks, made peace and happily

The Creek Indian; 1906.
(Image courtesy of Library of Congress)

traded with white neighbors. Others, called the Red Sticks, resented the invasion and refused to give up their lands.

An Indian Troublemaker

By the early 1800s, tensions were high when the Indian Chief, Tecumseh, traveled south to unite all native people. The legendary leader came from the Ohio region inhabited by Shawnee tribes. His father died young, and he was adopted by the Shawnee chief, Blackfish. Like Andrew Jackson, Tecumseh was a young teenager during the Revolutionary War. He saw his father and several siblings murdered by whites. Although a merciless warrior, he was respected for his disgust in torturing prisoners. It was one thing the native warrior wouldn't stand for.

By early 1800, Tecumseh was a well-known leader with a remarkable ability to give powerful, motivating speeches. Many Indians said he was a prophet. He cursed the white man for robbing his lands. At the same time, he made treaties with the British and criticized other chiefs who made peace with white settlers. By 1811, Tecumseh had traveled throughout many Indian villages encouraging tribes to unite in a war against all whites. He arrived just in time to rally the Creeks.

> **Fast Fact:** The Red Sticks came from the upper tribes of Creek Indians. They were named after their bright red war clubs and small, bundled matchsticks. The smaller sticks were used for counting days up to special events.

The Red Sticks began attacking Mississippi Territory settlements. Led by William Weatherford, their own half-white chief, they fought other Creeks that would not join them to eliminate the white men. In 1813, they launched an unexpected attack with an army of 700 warriors on Fort Mims, a big, fortified settlement just north of Mobile in what is today the state of Alabama.

Despite 45 militia men, the attack was over in four hours due to the onslaught of fiery, burning arrows. The Red Sticks violently killed over 200 of the 500 settlers living in the fort for safety, including women and children. The massacre was just the beginning of a bloody Indian war that would last a year and end in their defeat.

Orders to Indian Country

Tecumseh's war national cry forced Andrew Jackson from his recovery. He was still healing from his near fatal duel with Charles Dickinson. The bullet remained lodged in his arm. Despite the setback, Governor Blount of the Southwest Territory relayed the news that the President of the United States had called the militia to action. The wounded Jackson, now Major General Jackson, had no choice but to comply.

Born in North Carolina in 1749, William Blount remains one of Jackson's important political allies. The oldest of 13 children, Blount received a quality education that probably gave him the connections needed to serve in the North Carolina Legislature. He also attended the Constitutional Convention. He was a determined federalist and not afraid to voice his concerns over signing the Constitution. His reasoning for ultimately signing, he explained, was to keep the colonies unified and unanimous. During the Revolutionary War, he served as a paymaster, and afterward tried for the U.S. Senate. Like Jackson's early ambitions, he was not successful, so he headed west.

Once settled in the Appalachians, Blount worked with the Cherokees as he tried his hand at land speculating. Land speculating meant buying land while it was cheap and selling it at a higher price later when settlers arrived. His connections landed him the job as governor of the Southwest Territory after North Carolina changed its boundaries. This meant he welcomed the fresh-faced Andrew Jackson to town as a prosecutor when he arrived with his good friend, McNairy.

Despite being highly educated, experienced, and aristocratic, Blount and Jackson appear to have gotten along quite well. Not long after licensing Jackson to practice as an attorney, he appointed Jackson to serve on the board over the Davidson Academy School. Popular and well respected, Blount was a good mentor for the young lawyer. He not only exchanged favors, but he provided the influence and connections Jackson needed to get ahead.

For Blount, things took a turn for the worse in 1797. Tennessee was now a state, and he had the senate job he'd once wanted in North Carolina. Like Jackson, he was frustrated with the Spanish presence in Mississippi. Deciding to take matters into his own hands, Blount secretly began making deals with Indians and the British to get them out, but he accidentally hinted at his intentions in a letter that quickly found its way to officials.

President John Adams didn't want Blount to start a war with Spain, so the administration took action to remove him from the Senate for punishment. It didn't dissuade Tennesseans from loving Blount's ambitions to save their region of the country. The people, along with Jackson's vocal support, elected Blount right back to the Tennessee state senate. In return, Blount used his influence to help Jackson win the federal senate seat he'd lost.

William Blount passed on the President's orders for military action against the Creek Indians to Jackson. They often called on one another for favors, and Jackson never hesitated to use his connection with Blount to complain about his enemies. This time, however, there would be no influence or discussions. Major General Jackson rallied his fellow Tennesseans and took up his responsibility to serve as General. His job was to wipe out the Indians that had attacked Fort Mims. This response rang the starting bell for the Creek Indian Wars.

Murder and Massacre

The Creek Indian Wars were partially a consequence of a war called the War of 1812 between America and Great Britain. The Southwest Territory at that time included Georgia, Alabama, and Mississippi, as well as Blount and Jackson's home of Tennessee. It was the government's intention to form the Southwest Territory and take over Indian lands for white settlers. This would grow the nation and keep out foreign enemies. The Creek Nation, especially the stubborn Red Sticks, was in the way.

Even before the Fort Mims massacre, there were at least nine battles with the Red Sticks at places like Burnt Hole Creek and Holy Ground in today's eastern Alabama. The Indians were frustrated by the white settlements along their rivers, but they needed more weapons to fight. Reports trickled in to the militia that supplies were available for Indians in Pensacola, Florida, and that the Red Sticks had decided to travel there to get more guns. Their numbers were estimated to be around 300, and rumors spread that they beat up other Indians who wouldn't join them. They burned homes and farms of whites in their path.

Jackson quelling the mutiny
(Image courtesy of Library of Congress)

The Red Sticks made camp at a hill near a body of water called Burnt Corn Creek. Because some chose not to fight, they'd been run off, leaving the Indian army with less than 100 men. The American militia, hot on their trail, numbered around 180. They were able to surprise the Red Sticks and take their belongings, but while packing them up, the Red Sticks regrouped and charged them again.

To these Creek Indians, this clash meant war. Tribes had to decide where they stood in the fight for defending their lands. It was after this clash over weapons that the Red Sticks decided to attack Fort Mims.

With Jackson forced out of recovery from the Dickinson duel, the first thing he did was gather the troops. He called upon Tennessee volunteers to join him in defending their Nashville settlement from "invasion from the savage foe" so they wouldn't end up like the Americans at Fort Mims. The militia gathered 80 miles southward; despite his handicap, General Jackson promised to lead them in person.

They spent weeks chasing shadows and waging small battles before they caught up with the Red Sticks at Talladega. About 2,000 men under Jackson's command fought and chased off the Creeks into the mountains. Afterward, although it was seen as a victory, wounded soldiers and food shortages became a real problem.

Horses and supplies ran out. Men were hungry, cold, and wanted to go home. To those who threatened to leave, the fiery general declared, "I will quell mutiny and punish desertion!" At one point, he found it necessary to surround an abandoning brigade, a military unit, with cannons until they agreed to do their duty. Jackson and his army successfully wiped out the Indian villages of Tallasahatchee and Talladega.

A Friend for Life

One impressive member of General Jackson's Tennessee volunteers who would go on to become one of his best friends was a young man named Sam Houston. Born in 1793 in Virginia, he was between 20 and 21 years old at the time of the Creek Wars. He grew to be a large man, well over six feet tall.

Houston had plenty of experience with Native Americans. At 16, unhappy with his family circumstances, he ran away from home and lived with the Cherokees for three years. He became fluent in their language and was given the name Black Raven.

Houston crossed paths with Jackson when he enlisted to fight the British in the War of 1812. He eventually rose to third lieutenant and was transferred into a unit that joined General Jackson in his march to fight the Creeks. It didn't include fighting Cherokees, but it did include pay. It was during the famous battle at a beautiful place called Horseshoe Bend that he impressed the future president with his courage and endurance.

At Horseshoe Bend, as men rushed to climb the walls into the Red Stick fortress at their general's command, Houston took an arrow in the leg but kept going. He demanded that the surgeon jerk it out, barbs and all. He then rushed back into the fight when the call for volunteers came to weed out Creeks taking refuge behind logs. It took two bullets to put him out of action, but neither was fatal.

> In his own words, he remembered:
> *"The sun was going down, and it set on the ruin of the Creek nation. Where, but a few hours before a thousand brave... [warriors] had scowled on death and their assailants, there was nothing to be seen but volumes of dense smoke, rising heavily over the corpses of painted warriors, and the burning ruins of their fortifications"* (Brands, 2005).

Heaped with praise by his commanding officer, Houston took Jackson's advice and returned to Tennessee to study law. He moved forward into politics, becoming governor of Tennessee, but marriage and alcohol problems forced him to resign. He eventually fled to Texas, but not before marrying a Cherokee woman despite the social consequences.

Jackson remained Houston's political mentor and good friend all of his life. When Houston became commander of Texas armies, he used his valuable Creek War experience to beat back the Mexicans in 18 minutes. This victory brought Texas into the Union and made Houston a hero.

> A letter from President Jackson to Houston after this event shows the depth of the friendship:
> *"If providence spares me, to next summer of which I have great doubts, I hope to see you, your noble lady and charming boy at the Hermitage, where you will receive a hearty welcome... Accept the tender of the friend, salutation of myself and household to you and yours. Believe me your friend..."* (Brands, 2005).

Sam Houston went on to be the only governor of two different states. Besides governing Tennessee, he was elected governor of Texas in 1859. As a later senator, one funny story says he angrily flogged a congressman in the streets of Washington with a cane carved of wood from The Hermitage. He was fined instead of jailed, but he never paid it. The president, Andrew Jackson, later waived the penalty.

The lifelong friendship ended at Jackson's deathbed. Houston traveled anxiously to be at his friend's side but did not make it in time. Some claim the large Indian fighter fell over his general's body and sobbed. Others said he sat quietly on the bed beside the body and told his son, "...remember you have looked on the face of Andrew Jackson" (Marquis, 1988).

The Infamous Davy Crockett

Another popular figure that fought under General Jackson's command was Davy Crockett. Unlike Sam Houston, Crockett and Jackson weren't the best of friends. They had similar backgrounds, though. Crockett was born in the Appalachian Mountains in eastern Tennessee. His father loaned him out to farmers for work so he had little time for schooling. After his father died, he worked with his brothers awhile before taking off at 16 years old. He would spend the rest of his life making his way west looking for land and trying to make a living.

Crockett probably heard about the militia and opportunity for pay around the time General Jackson rounded up volunteers to fight the Creeks. Although Crockett eventually rose in the ranks to become a sergeant, he didn't like military life. During the Creek Wars, he acted as a scout, riding ahead of the troops to look for Indians. He fought at Talladega under Jackson, but when the hunger strike caused an angry mutiny, he joined a group of soldiers that rebelled and was allowed to return home. War was too bloody and savage to Crockett. Despite his infamous reputation for bear hunting, it was his first experience at war.

Crockett returned to Tennessee where he served in the legislature and House of Representatives after the Creek Wars. He was friendly with Sam Houston, but he and Jackson had political differences. He lost his last election in 1835 to Jackson's party.

> He said to his supporters:
>
> *"My friends, I suppose you all are aware that I was recently a candidate for Congress. I told the voters that if they would elect me I would serve them to the best of my ability; but if they did not, they might go to hell, and I would go to Texas. I am on my way now"* (Hutton, 1999).

Crockett moved on to Texas and eventually fought General Santa Anna for Texas independence. His colorful political career made him a famous storyteller, bear hunter, friend of the Cherokees, sharp shooter, and friend to the common man. He died a hero at the Alamo in San Antonio, Texas, on March 6, 1838, when Mexican forces overran the pueblo mission.

 Fast Fact: The Alamo was a small pueblo mission, or religious building, in San Antonio, Texas. Surrounded by cottonwood trees, it was the tragic location of a battle against Mexico for Texas independence in 1838. Because the Texans were outnumbered, defeated, and some executed, "Remember the Alamo!" became a famous war cry.

The Indian Prince

If Andrew Jackson was the heart and soul of the Tennessee Militia, the chief of the Creek Nation, born as William Weatherford, played the same role for the Creek Indians. He was from just north of today's Montgomery, Alabama, and his father was a white Scottish trader named Charles. His mother was a Creek Indian princess called Sahoy. Weatherford chose his mother's way of life.

When the great Indian leader, Tecumseh, came from the North and encouraged all Indians to fight for their lands, Weatherford must have agreed with this idea. It was a call to return to the old ways. A problem quickly developed, however. His people began to fight amongst themselves.

The Red Sticks were jealous of other Creeks who were friendly with whites. They seemed better off economically and had begun to embrace the modern way of life. This started the civil war within the Creek Nation that would send the Red Sticks to Pensacola to get more war supplies. They took the American attack on their party as a declaration for war, and it was afterward they attacked Fort Mims.

Weatherford led the attack on the massacre on the settlement, although witnesses say he pled for discipline and restraint among his warriors. He later claimed he had nothing to do with the horrific deaths of whites, blacks, and friendly Indians that day.

Jackson and his Tennessee Militia probably assumed Weatherford would be at the Red Stick defensive village he helped build some months before the final Creek battle at Horseshoe Bend. He was not. The army had chased him and his mystical reputation for some time. Soldiers told a story of how he once jumped his horse off a giant, rocky cliff and landed far below in a river to easily swim away. At the time, he appeared to be undefeatable, but the attack at Horseshoe Bend had far reaching consequences for Weatherford that Jackson may have never predicted.

The Bloody Battle of Horseshoe Bend

The beginning of the end for the Creek Nation occurred at Horseshoe Bend on March 27, 1813. Major General Jackson and his men had chased William Weatherford, the Creeks, and the Red Stick chief, Menawa, for months with little success.

When news came that the Red Sticks had gathered for their final defense at a meeting of the Tallapoosa and Coosa Rivers, the General and his more than 3,000 men cut a trail over 50 miles through the forest in three days.

When they arrived, the scene took them by surprise. The native fortifications at Horseshoe Bend were impressive and dangerous.

> To Governor Blount, he wrote:
> *"This bend resembles in its curvature that of a horse shoe, and is thence called by that name among the whites. Nature furnishes few situations so eligible for defence; and barbarians have never rendered one more secure by art. Across the neck of land which leads into it from the North, they had erected a breastwork, of greatest compactness and strength — from five to eight feet high, and prepared with double rows of port-holes very artfully arranged. The figure of this wall, manifested no less skill in the projectors of it, than its construction: an army could not approach it without being exposed to a double and cross fire from the enemy who lay in perfect security behind it"*
> (Brands, 2005).

👉 **Fast Fact:** *At this time, the land around Horseshoe Bend was part of the eastern Mississippi Territory. Today, the grounds are a national military park in Alabama, not far from the Georgia border. With no signs of the dreadful war there anymore, it's a quiet and beautiful meadow alongside a river that visitors can enjoy. The river circles the high meadow in the shape of a horseshoe.*

At first, it seemed a daunting task to attack a defense that could fire from all directions. The militia camped six miles away from their enemies the evening of March 27th. Again, Jackson rallied his men with the encouragement to "Let every shot tell!" He also firmly promised them death if they retreated from their posts. Even though older and more experienced than in his wild lawyer days, the general firmly believed every man must

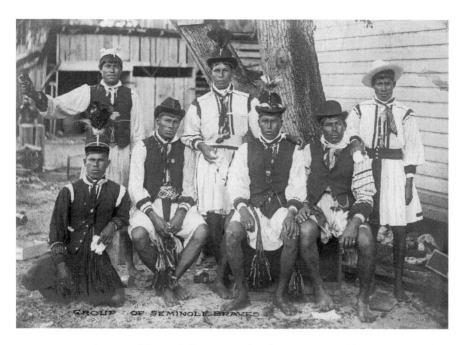

A group of Seminole braves; posed and wearing native dress.
(Photo courtesy of Library of Congress)

do his duty — even to the death. He did not want to capture the Indian fortress; he wanted to destroy them.

The battle began mid-morning. General Jackson realized that he actually had the advantage, because he could surround the Indians. He sent his second in command, John Coffee, to cross the river downstream to attack the rear. Coffee had over 1,000 mounted infantry, or men on horseback, under his command. He also had Lower Creek allies. Jackson called his Tennessee volunteers and prepared to attack the front lines of the peninsula. They began with cannon fire from two cannons positioned just 80 yards from the enemy's walls. Within were approximately 1,000 Red Sticks, including some women and children.

The cannon fire did its job and distracted the Red Sticks from the militia creeping up behind them. This was lucky, as Coffee later reported that their Lower Creek and Cherokee friends crashed across the river to attack and steal canoes from those who might try to escape on the water.

At the front barricade, arrows and gunfire were exchanged. When the order was given, the militia rushed the fortification, and pushed their own guns through the holes in the fort that the Indians were using to fire through. They fired back at point blank range. One witness reported the heat became so terrible that musket balls shot from the enemy stuck to the hot barrels of the soldier's guns.

The attack from the front and rear threw the Red Sticks into confusion. It gave Jackson's men the opportunity to climb the fort walls and open the gates. Hundreds of white men poured into the Red Sticks last line of defense. The Indians were cut down mercilessly. Those who tried to escape the river only found death, so many so that the river was strewn with over 300 bodies, and the water ran red. As the battle continued to move south toward late afternoon, a few survivors managed to barricade themselves behind a riverbank at dusk. By morning, the last of the Creeks were dead or taken prisoner.

The battle was finished.

Few of the Creeks survived. Chief Menawa escaped, but over 1,000 of his warriors lay dead. In contrast, General Jackson lost only 49 men including his Indian allies. Hundreds on both sides were critically wounded.

> To Governor Blount he wrote,
>
> "...twenty six white men killed and one hundred and seven wounded Cherokees, eighteen killed, and thirty six wounded, friendly Creeks Five killed and eleven wounded. The loss of Col. Williams' reg't of Regulars is seventeen killed and fifty five wounded; three of whom have since died. Among the former were Major Montgomery, Lieut' Somerville, and Lieut' Moulton, who, fell in the charge which was made on the works. No men ever acted more gallantly, or fell more gloriously" (Correspondence of Andrew Jackson, 1814).

Following the battle, General Jackson had no way to know if the fighting had ended or not. William Weatherford was still on the loose. He had not been at the Red Stick fort on the day of the battle. Many of the Red Sticks had disappeared into the forests where their women and children were hiding. No one came forth to surrender or plead for peace. Jackson thought there would be more battles. His militia searched the remaining villages but found them empty. It's recorded that in one, they found scalps from the Fort Mims Massacre and gave them an appropriate burial.

The Major General returned with his men to nearby Fort Jackson. He confidently wrote to his Rachel, "The fiends of Tallapoosa will no longer murder our women and children." Jackson didn't have long to wait before he realized the degree of his success. Weeks after the slaughter at Horseshoe Bend, a strange half-white, half-native man walked in without ropes or chains. William Weatherford, also called Red Eagle, felt forced to surrender.

According to Weatherford, he had no more warriors, and the widows and children were starving and afraid. Slowly dying, the remainder of his people demanded that he ask for peace. To onlookers, he appeared depressed and forlorn. He didn't care what would be done to him; he wanted only protection for those who lived. "I am in your power," he told the General.

Jackson chose not to execute him that day. Whether he was impressed by his noble figure and dignity, or he believed the chieftain would convince the rest of the Red Sticks to surrender, Weatherford walked away a free man.

Later on August 9, 1814, the Creek Indian War came to an official close as the remaining Creek chiefs reluctantly signed the Treaty of Fort Jackson. For the punishment of their Red Stick brothers' actions, the Upper and Lower Creeks gave up over 20 million acres of land. Any hope they would be rewarded for being allies were forgotten when General Jackson, known by now as "Sharp Knife" and "Mad Dog Jackson," made it clear to any who would not agree that they would be treated as enemies and not provided with any desperately needed food.

Today, the land surrendered by the Creeks is almost one half the State of Alabama and includes a large part of the southwestern region of Georgia. It was the most decisive victory over any American Indians up to that point in history.

Into the Swamps

The surrender of the Creeks did not end Indian problems in the southern Unites States. In 1818, Spain controlled Florida, and the Seminole Indian activity that hurt white settlers spilled over into the United States territory. This was a problem for the American government, but also an opportunity. The new John Adams presidential administration had its eye on Florida but didn't want to start a war. Andrew Jackson, they knew, just might be the key to getting what they wanted.

The name *Seminole* is believed to come from a Creek word that means "runaway." Other historians suspect it may come from an old Spanish word for "wild." Regardless, as white settlers began to cross from the Southwest Territory into their lands, the Seminole Indians felt obligated to run them out for a change.

> **Fast Fact:** The Seminoles were believed to have mixed with older Creek tribes who fled into the lower swamps of the continent to escape Europeans. They built villages in the Everglade swamps of Florida. They also hunted, fished, and grew crops. Their homes could be log cabins or thatched shelters called chickees.

The President of the United States, James Monroe, sent orders to Jackson, who was resting at the Hermitage, that the militia was needed again. The general was ordered to conquer Indians on the attack and recapture slaves who routinely escaped to Florida to join Seminoles and live as free men. The instructions were vague. In between the lines, the letter suggested it might be an opportunity to seize Florida for the United States.

*An imaginative portrayal of an event in the Texas war of independence.
Santa Anna, his brother-in-law General Martin Perfecto de Cos,
and Samuel Houston are shown after the Battle of San Jacinto in late April
1836. Houston is holding a musket, the most popular weapon of the time.
(Image courtesy of Library of Congress)*

General Jackson took the hint. He left Tennessee in 1818 with a force of 1,000 men armed with Springfield muskets and their attached, knife-like bayonets. They marched first to a Negro fort on the Apalachicola River supplied by the British and watched gunships blow it up. Jackson rebuilt the fort and named it Fort Gadsden. From there, he marched to St. Marks, a Spanish garrison (fort), and ordered them to surrender because they had been helping local Seminoles. The Spanish gave it up without a fight.

Along their march, the militia fought the Seminoles in one skirmish after another. Often, the warriors would leave their villages undefended, and the militia would march in and burn them down. This was an easier tactic than a long battle. In one fight, they captured a white man named Alexander Arbuthnot. He was a British subject and friend of the Seminoles. Jackson accused him of helping them fight the Americans and had him arrested.

> 👉 **Fast Fact:** *The weapon of the day, the popular musket, took a long time to load — 10 arrows could be shot before a gun could be fired. The sharp bayonets on the end of the muskets were the soldiers' only real weapons in close hand-to-hand combat with Indians.*

Next, the march took the army to the land of Billy Bowlegs. The Indians were warned in advance, and the village was found abandoned. Another prisoner, a British solider and native of Nassau in the Bahamas Islands, was also captured while aiding the enemy. His name was Robert Armbrister.

With many Seminoles killed or captured, General Jackson returned to Fort Gadsden with his prisoners. His passionate belief that any enemy against the United States should be punished motivated him to hold a trial for the white men, Arbuthnot and Armbrister. Although he had no legal right, Jackson ordered them to a court with no representation and found them guilty.

Arbuthnot was hanged. After some arguments, Armbrister was sentenced to 50 lashes, and he had to wear an iron ball and chain for a year. That didn't sit well with Jackson's idea of punishment. To everyone's shock, he overturned the sentence and had him shot.

The militia wasn't finished with Florida after the executions. General Jackson ordered them back into formation to hunt down the remaining Seminoles and escaped slaves with his eye toward the governing beach town of Pensacola. The Spanish controlled Florida with only a few garrisons. They did not control the Seminoles and had ignored the United States' requests for protecting their citizens.

Jackson felt this irresponsibility created grounds for self-defense, and he marched into Pensacola chasing the Spanish eastward into a stone fortress called Fort Barrancas. The next morning, he used his cannons to rain down gunfire when they wouldn't surrender, and he took out the Spanish in one day.

In the letter to the president, he reported he had conquered the Indians and removed all foreign interferences, ultimately taking the land of Florida for the United States.

Not that he'd been asked to do it.

Andrew Jackson, with the Tennessee forces, on the Hickory Grounds.
(Photo courtesy of Library of Congress)

Chapter Six: The Story Behind "Old Hickory"

The War of 1812 was a shadow just ahead on the horizon. At one point, General Jackson's troops were ordered from Florida to New Orleans, but the orders were confusing, and the men needed supplies. Jackson returned to Nashville against the command, determined to use his friends and credit if necessary to feed and clothe his soldiers before waging war on anyone.

His bosses were furious, but not the militia. Admiringly, the men began calling him "Old Hickory," because like a branch from the sturdy tree, he was impossible to break. It was the first to come of many nicknames, but Old Hickory stuck and endured long after his death.

Across the ocean, England was busy, too. The British were at war, trying to keep Napoleon Bonaparte from invading with his French armies. England needed men to sail their ships, so whenever Royal Navy frigates felt the Americans were breaking trade agreements at sea, they boarded American vessels and kidnapped their sailors in return.

Fast Fact: *Thousands of American sailors were forced to sail under the British flag, a tradition called impressment, which England had practiced on its own people for hundreds of years. In 1807, a British warship fired on the American naval frigate, Chesapeake, and took four sailors. It almost started a war.*

The Unites States prohibited any trade with Britain or France. This did little to help tensions, because British forces on the Canadian border teamed up with Indians and supplied them with weapons to fight settlers. After several small battles between American forces and British Redcoats in the north, the United States president, James Madison, ordered Congress to meet. To England's surprise, America declared war on June 18,1812, just as General Jackson was battling the Creek Indians.

England continued to fight for land on the Canadian border and sent ships to block American ports so no one could sail in or out. A year later, they defeated Bonaparte in Europe and turned their full attention to re-taking American lands. The city of Washington was captured and burned. Redcoats moved on to Baltimore, but they were overpowered there and beaten back.

Relentless, England set its sights on the southern city of New Orleans at the bottom corner of the American territory. To their surprise, the Indian fighter, Andrew Jackson, would meet them at the mouth of the Mississippi River.

The Battle of New Orleans

If the War of 1812 began as a second revolution, the Battle of New Orleans slammed the door on the British attempt to control the Mississippi River, American trade, and Westward expansion. They had battled the Americans at the Canadian border, and they had attacked and burned Washington. Now, England turned its attention to claiming Louisiana for itself.

Occupied in Florida, General Jackson was busy keeping the Indians under control and the Spanish and British out. The Americans still did not have total control of that territory. Completely unafraid by the fighting in Florida, the Redcoats and Royal Navy began to inch their way toward New Orleans by attacking east at Mobile. American forces counterattacked at nearby Fort Bowyer, and the British ships failed to take over and win the bay.

At the same time Mobile was under threat, a letter from New Orleans arrived for Jackson. It pleaded with the general to march to their city at the

General Andrew Jackson on horseback commanding troops in battle against the British; January 8, 1815. (Photo courtesy of Library of Congress)

mouth of the Mississippi and protect them. He departed in November with around 1,000 men. The weather would be one of the coldest on record in Louisiana when the Redcoats arrived. There, they would find the swamps freezing and slippery.

> 👉 **Fast Fact:** *In 1814, New Orleans was a city with mixed loyalties. Full of Frenchmen, Spaniards, Indians, free blacks, and even pirates, the citizens didn't really feel like they were a part of the United States. It was swampy country, lined by the gulf coast due south, and riddled with lakes, rivers, and marshes. Waterfowl were everywhere. So were mosquitoes and the terrifying American alligator.*

General Jackson arrived in New Orleans and set city leaders straight right away. His men would not take on the thousands of British soldiers alone. He declared martial law, set curfews, and ordered men of every race, culture, and class to join the militia. While they prepared, the British wasted no time landing nearby at Lake Borgne. Within days, they defeated the American gunboats there.

One early asset the British hoped to have on their side was the notorious and local pirate Jean Lafitte. Lafitte and his brother led a band of pirates on the nearby islands in Barataria Bay. The buccaneers smuggled slaves and goods on the black market, making enemies of the businessmen in New Orleans. The Royal Navy knew their knowledge of the coast and gunnery skills would come in handy.

On September 3, a Captain Lockyer of the *HMS Sophia* visited Lafitte and offered him a deal: fight the Americans or be destroyed by the Royal Navy. Lafitte somewhat agreed. He asked for two weeks to think about the rewards of being made a captain and the large prize of $30,000. During this time, he sent the information to New Orleans and offered the governor, William Claiborne, his help. Claiborne refused and sent ships to destroy the den of thieves.

Unsuccessful, Lafitte next approached Andrew Jackson. The general didn't want a criminal's assistance and almost refused, but he knew the pirates of Lafitte had skills and supplies his army would need. He granted the pirates a pardon and enlisted their help. By December, with canals dug, ramparts built, and more troops added to the ragtag army of men of every color and creed, the Americans were as ready as they would ever be.

The British landed on the Bayou Bienvenu on December 22, 1814. They had used barges to unload their ships on Lake Borgne. Besides over 7,000 soldiers, there were horses, weapons, and artillery ready to make war. Within a day, they captured the plantation of Jacques Villerè, who commanded the local militia before Jackson arrived. His son managed to escape and sound the warning. That night, the militia made its first attack.

The American forces learned a great deal from fighting Indians. They weren't above stealth and trickery. An armed gunship was sent upriver to fire on British troops who were easy marks as they sat around bright campfires trying to stay warm. American infantry fired artillery from different vantage points in the trees, practically invisible in the dark. There was hand-to-hand combat at some point during the night, and by morning, the Redcoats counted nearly 250 of their men down. They never expected the Americans to respond right away, much less after dark.

Several small battles occurred over the next two weeks. On January 1st, the British attacked with artillery guns for three hours until they ran out of ammunition. They destroyed several American cannons and supplies. General Jackson knew it was only a matter of time before a full-scale attack. After attacking the Redcoats on the Villerè plantation, he set his sights on reinforcing the Rodriguez Canal for the final battle.

The Americans' defensive canal, a waterway, was 10 feet wide but needed to be widened. Using slave labor, the militia turned the canal into a mile long, dirt-filled trench. They built it up seven feet high and lined it with timber and cotton bales. The canal led into a cypress-filled swamp, and eight artillery batteries would protect it. Always confident when addressing his men, General Jackson promised they would drive the "red-coat rascals" into either the river or the swamps.

On January 8th, the final battle began at dawn. Strangely, the treaty to end the war had already been signed in Europe on December 24th, but word had not come, so the War of 1812 continued on in New Orleans. Determined, the British hoped to attack in darkness and take advantage of a fog, but because of setbacks, the sun rose. Mists lifted as the Redcoats attacked both the east and west banks in plain sight.

As the British lines advanced to fire their weapons on the mile long rampart, or wall, the general's forces easily cut them down with cannon and gunfire. Despite the enormous number of British soldiers, they could not reach the Americans. They were so unprepared that they had even forgotten the ladders needed to climb the dirt walls once they reached them.

One survivor described the ammunition from the American rampart as looking like fiery furnaces. The fight ended within a half hour, and it left the ground "littered' with dead and dying Redcoats. The British retreated, and a ceasefire was granted. Three British generals and seven colonels were among the dead.

The pirates of Lafitte were crucial when it came to gunnery skills during the battle. Although Laffite and his brother were not positioned on the west bank, many of their men were, and they fought under the direction of General Jackson. For their service, the president of the United States officially pardoned the entire band of pirates as promised. They were allowed to return to life at sea afterward.

Lafitte moved on to Texas, where he went back to attacking Spanish ships. In 1820, after some of his men accidentally boarded American vessels, he abandoned the coast for South America in his own ship, *The Pride*. Many believe he disappeared back into the life of piracy on the high seas.

The British abandoned the quest for New Orleans, and Major General Andrew Jackson became a true national hero. He had chased the Indians deep into the Florida swamps. He'd managed to claim Florida for the Union, and he secured Louisiana and trade on the Mississippi River for the rest of the country. In fact, he had closed the last chapter on England's attempt to strangle the growth and power of the United States through bloodshed.

Although Jackson worried about the lurking Royal Navy in the Gulf and wouldn't consider the fight over until it was official, the War of 1812 finally ended with the ratifying of the Treaty of Ghent in mid-February by the Senate. It was 1815.

The March on Pensacola

While the president and people of the United States were celebrating the likely possession of Florida thanks to the Major General, Jackson's enemies complained about his habit of doing his own thing without formal orders. As was his way, the Indian fighter had made decisions and issued commands without direct instructions from the president.

Jackson returned to the Hermitage more popular than ever. Some compared him to George Washington. Traveling east, he was honored at dinners and parties. He visited Monticello, the home of Thomas Jefferson, and was congratulated on his successful campaign.

The next few years, he tried to find peace at the Hermitage with Rachel, but politics would not let him be. His enemies wanted him punished. Spain refused to ratify the treaty to relinquish Florida. The question of slavery and what was to be done began to divide the north and south. The country suffered a financial banking crisis that affected his friends and troops, and above all, he now struggled to regain his seriously failing health.

 Fast Fact: Monticello was the home of Thomas Jefferson in southern Virginia. It was built in the Classical Revival style with Roman influences. It included three stories of 35 rooms, giant windows, and a dome on the roof. The house was full of inventions that were new ideas at the time. Some included a great clock with two faces, a revolving bookstand, the hideaway bed, and a turning machine for hanging clothes. Today, Monticello is a national park welcoming visitors from around the world.

President James Monroe knew it would be safest for everyone if Old Hickory could be forced into retirement. That way, they could avoid a public trial and the anger of the American people who loved him. With Spain almost ready to concede the lands in Florida, the president thought it best to send down the man who had captured it — Andrew Jackson. It would be a great honor for Jackson to be officially handed over Florida, and it would be the last assignment before he retired.

Rachel joined her husband for the exciting event, traveling with him to New Orleans and and then to Pensacola to meet the Spanish governor. They found Pensacola as beautiful as ever, with soft white sand and crystal turquoise waters. After the Spanish flag came down and the American flag fluttered in the cool breezes, General Jackson claimed it was his now his right to preside and govern there.

He wasn't shy about pressuring the Spanish to leave quickly. At one point, he and the former Spanish leader, José María Callava almost came to blows during a shouting match over the paperwork of a request from a former Spanish citizen. Neither man spoke the other's language, which left a translator, and ultimately a judge, in the middle of it. By the time Jackson felt it was safe and dignified enough to return to his Hermitage, Spain surrendered for good, and the new officials of American Florida had experienced a taste of the temper, control, and stubbornness of General Jackson.

Sickness and Soldiering

No one knows exactly why Andrew Jackson spent the majority of his life ill. As a boy, he was described as being skinny and pale. He somehow survived the smallpox he caught in the Revolutionary prison camp, but he never fully regained or lived a healthy life. Some historians believe he may have lived with stomach parasites common even in North Carolina, that he could have caught from poor food, tainted water, or living circumstances around other people and animals.

Fast Fact: Medicine in the 1700 and 1800s was very different than it is today. Although doctors were respected, they still didn't understand germs and bacteria. Some of the most popular drugs, like arsenic and lead, were actually poisonous and killed patients.

Besides living with almost constant stomach and intestinal problems, Jackson complained as early as 1798 of suffering from rheumatism after injuring his knee. He nearly caught pneumonia after rescuing horses on a winter night without being properly dressed. With the bullet in his wounded arm, Jackson fought the Creek Wars hardly able to write or feed himself. At times, he would feel so sick he would just sit and command from his bed.

The bullet left over from his duel with Charles Dickinson probably contributed to his illnesses. It could've caused a serious infection that his body would have constantly fought back with low fevers. The bullet, made of lead, may have poisoned him. His illnesses of cramps, pain, and other problems shared symptoms with lead poisoning. Whatever health problems he had been born with, fighting outdoors with a bullet lodged permanently in his body only made things that much worse.

Jackson's illness grew serious in Florida. While governing in Pensacola, he suffered severe digestion troubles that made him as thin and gaunt as ever. He wrote a friend that he suffered from dysentery for almost four months. Even upon returning to the Hermitage intending to retire, the change in diet, which meant more and better quality food, did not solve his health problems. By the time he turned 54 years old, he didn't think he'd live much longer.

Although sickly, Jackson did survive long enough to become president. He drank alcohol and coffee, which may have protected him from some water-born illnesses. Witnesses noticed that his limbs would often swell despite the best care from doctors. His medicines later in life probably in-cluded opiates, which helped in some ways, but he continued to decline.

In the end, he suffered from shortness of breath, pain in his sides, poor eyesight, and frequent chills and fevers. These final health issues took his life just as America and his dear friend Sam Houston chased General Santa Anna out of Texas for good.

(Image courtesy of Library of Congress)

Chapter Seven:
The Journey to the White House

Letters from friends and supporters flooded into Tennessee after Jackson returned from Florida and embraced retirement. He ignored the suggestion that presidential candidate William Crawford would win if someone more popular didn't run against him. Crawford acted as Secretary of the Treasury for President Monroe, but he didn't agree with his policies. He had other ideas — opinions that many found threatening.

Jackson tried to focus on his own problems. The Hermitage struggled in the poor economy. Prices for cotton and corn were up and down, and there was a drought. He did his best to manage the estate and care for his family while battling health problems, but politics would not leave him alone.

Even his close friend, Sam Houston, reminded him of his duty to his country and the dangers of continuing the Virginia tradition of aristocratic presidents and practices. The pressure didn't help. Two years before the next election, the lawmakers of Tennessee informed Jackson that they intended to nominate him as a presidential candidate. They next elected him to the Senate. On his reluctant return to Washington, he drew crowds of attention and support. Slowly, Jackson accepted his destiny.

Four other men would compete for the White House:

1. William Crawford
2. Henry Clay, Speaker of the House of Representatives
3. John C. Calhoun, Secretary of War
4. John Quincy Adams, served as Secretary of State

Did You Know? These four men were all members of the Democratic-Republican Party known as Jeffersonians. Founded by Thomas Jefferson, these politicians believed in the power of common people and the idea that everyone should have a voice rather than rely on the upper class leadership of the Federalists. At the time, there were no other organized parties, and so they mattered little.

Again, Jackson found Washington boring, and he missed his Rachel. He was not opposed to the idea of someone else winning the election besides Crawford. Of him, he said, "I would support the devil first." Crawford was thought to be an imposing man with a weakness for being uncivil and insensitive. He spoke well and was popular among the people of Virginia, but his political equals disliked him.

Like Jackson, settlers in the southwest region did not like Crawford either. They felt the country needed Jackson's leadership, confidence, and ability to make swift, courageous decisions. John Calhoun surrendered his intentions to run as president quickly. That left John Quincy Adams with the support of New England and Henry Clay with the Ohio region.

In 1823, news came that Harrisburg, Pennsylvania, had nominated Jackson as their man. This showed other parts of the country were interested in the general. The race looked real and possible, but it would be a serious challenge for Jackson's reputation as a harsh and unbendable man. Unlike his competition, he didn't have a pedigree, a remarkable education, or years of experience overseas or in Washington. Although he had served briefly in Congress, the highlights of his career were mostly just military service and battle.

The 1824 Presidential Race

Leading up to the election of 1824, there was little campaigning in the public eye. A poorly organized and inefficient caucus of 1824 chose Crawford as the frontrunner. A caucus is a meeting where members of a party choose their candidate. Outside of his Tennessee supporters, it didn't appear that Jackson was much of a threat after the caucus. The other candidates didn't worry too much about him.

At work in Washington, Jackson was a humble senator who rarely spoke up. He made peace with many of his old enemies and avoided confrontations. The only controversy that stirred during the election months was a tariff, or tax proposal, to pay the national debt and help with the country's defenses. Feeling it necessary, Jackson quietly voted in support of the unpopular tax and then returned home for the summer.

The Major General was the outsider at election time, or so everyone thought. Concerned about his growing popularity, Crawford's supporters attacked Jackson, and Adams and Clay followed their example. It was too late. Jackson won a popular vote, beating Adams who was now the frontrunner by 50,000 votes. Besides his own territory, he'd had the support of the North and South Carolinas, Pennsylvania, and New Jersey. In a shocking victory, he took the electoral vote 99 to 84.

> **Fast Fact:** *The Constitution established the Electoral College to balance the election of a President between a vote in Congress and a popular vote of competent citizens called the electoral vote. The Electoral College has 538 electors. Each state has a number of electors that equals its members in Congress. When people vote in the popular vote, they are voting for their state's candidate's electors.*

At this time, a candidate had to win the majority of electoral votes, but results were split between Jackson and Adams, with Crawford and Clay coming in far behind at third and fourth. The decision now fell to the House of Representatives. Under the Twelfth Amendment at that time, each state would provide a delegation to submit one vote for the top three winning candidates.

Henry Clay was Speaker of the House of Representatives. He used his power to publically criticize Jackson's wild and unpredictable reputation. He accused him of being a "military chieftain" and stood behind Adams for president. In a controversial conclusion, the House voted in John Quincy Adams for president, and in return, Adams chose Clay as Secretary of State. Keeping with the tradition of the old aristocrats, another Secretary of State became president, and Clay had bargained his way into the vacant position.

Afterward, Jackson made the rounds of political parties for the outgoing president and the president-elect. He shook hands with the new leader of America and conducted himself in a calm and respectable way that

Henry and Lucretia Clay (Photo courtesy of Library of Congress)

surprised his critics. In private, however, he raged about the corruption of his peers. Though he had never aspired to be president, he felt robbed. The voice of the people had not been heard after all. The Jackson crowd in Washington and abroad in the countrysides of America immediately began to prepare for the next election.

The 1828 Campaign

After the 1824 election, the fury and bitterness of Jackson's supporters went from a simmer to full boil. Mudslinging knew no bounds. No one in the public eye was safe. The president, John Quincy Adams, knew he was unpopular. Some felt he chose controversial policies in order to improve his image. These included supporting transportation subsidies and new tariffs to encourage development. He couldn't do enough to make people happy, so he was continually attacked in the papers.

Fast Fact: Mudslinging is an expression to describe the personal attacks of one competitor against another by using insulting or scandalous information whether it's true or not. Today, it is still used to describe negative campaigning in politics.

Before President Adams even moved into the White House, a Nashville newspaper predicted Jackson would run in the next election of 1828. He had support in the House of Representatives. John Randolph, a fiery politician who had supported Thomas Jefferson, stood up to Secretary of State Henry Clay and President Adams, and their dirty deals. He called them out from the Senate, labeling them "puritans" and "Blacklegs." Clay was so angry that he challenged the famous Randolph to a duel; it ultimately resulted in nothing more than purposely missed shots.

Jackson also felt he had Thomas Jefferson's support. The former president and signer of the Declaration of Independence made it known from his sick bed that he was not satisfied with the current administration in Washington. This didn't go over well with Jackson's enemies. They began to attack Jackson's career decisions of the past, and worse, they went after his family.

> " In regards to being accused of being a military chieftain, Jackson had a ready response for a man who had never been in battle:
>
> *"...having the commission of Major General of militia in Tennessee, I made an appeal to the patriotism of the western citizens, when 3000 of them went with me to the field, to support her Eagles. If this can constitute me a 'military chieftain,' I am one"* (Brands, 2005).

This didn't stop the papers. Critics went after him for his shortcomings, his involvement in slavery, and as a last resort, they targeted Rachel and the confusion over the end of her first marriage. Jackson was accused of stealing another man's wife. Rachel was labeled a "dirty, black wench." The accusations and insults nearly broke Rachel's heart. She wanted nothing to do with politics or Washington. The cruelty sent Jackson into a frustrated depression.

As the Adams administration focused on new programs while bashing Andrew and Rachel's lives, Jackson supporters focused on the dishonesty of Washington and new ideas of democracy. Popular figures began to cross over to his side. Vice President James C. Calhoun gave Jackson the nod. Former supporters of Clay and Crawford joined up, too.

All the while, there were rallies, speeches, and papers exaggerating or lying about Jackson's ability to serve as the next president. He notably responded in defense of Rachel's reputation that truth would prevail. By the time of the 1828 election, he had the West, the South, and much of Washington behind him.

President Adams' supporters, who wanted him to serve a second term as president, could only focus on the past. They pointed out again and again that Jackson was violent and had no respect for authority. He was compared to Napoleon, and it was prophesied he would ruin the country everyone's ancestors had fought so hard to win.

When it came time to vote, no one seemed to care about the Jacksons' colorful past and reputations. General Jackson won the popular vote against Adams 647 to 508. He won the electoral vote 178 to 83. New York and Pennsylvania had sided with the Southwest, and Andrew Jackson became the oldest president to serve in the country's history. He was first to be born in a log cabin to immigrant parents. He was the first to be voted in by the voice of the people.

Inaugurated

President Jackson didn't have long to celebrate his victory. The toll of the campaign weighed heavy on Rachel. She worried about her country girl image in the White House. Although she dreaded the move, she decided that it was her duty to support her husband and prepare herself for four years of examination and criticism.

On December 18th, not long before they were supposed to leave, she complained of violent chest pains, and a doctor was called to the house. Jackson refused to leave her side, even as the new leader of the United States.

She died four days later, and Jackson held on to her up until her funeral. Her remains were pried from his grieving arms.

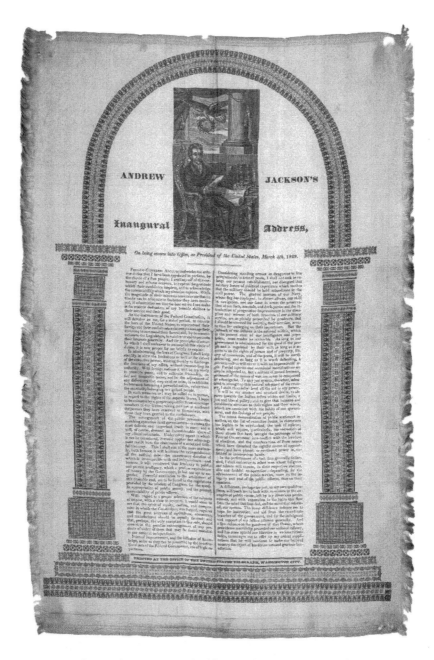

Andrew Jackson's inaugural address, on being sworn into office, as President of the United States, March 4, 1829. Printed at the office of the United States Telegraph. (Image courtesy of Library of Congress)

Arriving in Washington on February 15th, there were only a few weeks for the new president to prepare for his inauguration at a hotel. Thousands of people flooded into Washington on wagons, carts, and by foot. Their excitement could not be contained. Finally, on the morning of March 4th, Jackson set out for the Capitol building overwhelmed by crowds. Bands played a tune written for him after the Battle of New Orleans. There was a 24-gun salute. He sat with the senate while new members were sworn in.

At noon, the senate adjourned, and he made his way through growing crowds toward the White House for his own oath. With glasses perched atop his head, he repeated the oath in soft tones, kissed the Bible, and then bowed to the crowd in an act of humility. Although mourning deeply for his Rachel, he would not let the people down.

Scores of commoners of every social class and color followed the president into the White House reception. A long-standing tradition opened the president's home to visitors after each inauguration. This party had no guest list. Everyone was welcome, and so the numbers quickly became uncontrollable. Witnesses estimated he shook over 10,000 hands.

Food and punch went first and fast. Anything made of glass, including china, was shattered. There was fighting among the men and fainting among the women. The property looked like a battle scene. A day later, critics complained at what the new administration had allowed to take place at the most respectable address in the nation. The people of Andrew Jackson were labeled filthy rabble and commoners. In the long run, however, the poor judgment and behavior of the rejoicing crowds for the new president had no serious effect.

The people had spoken.

Chapter Eight: The Presidency

The American people loved their new president. The city of Washington was terrified. Andrew Jackson was on a mission to repair the damage that had been done to America's democratic ideas by social class or carelessness. He would weed out the old public officers who had been in government too long. During his first year in office, three expressions came to define him and his first administration: The Spoils System, the Kitchen Cabinet, and the Petticoat Affair.

Some politicians in Washington felt President Jackson's election was the beginning of a reign of terror, and they were right. He'd not only stolen President Adam's dreams of a second term, but he was now getting rid of political enemies by replacing them with friends. The press called President Jackson's firing and hiring decisions "The Spoils System." Critics accused him of rewarding all of his defenders and personal friends.

Jackson received many letters from angry wives and friends about the people he fired, but it didn't bother him. Instead, he announced his intention to change government service by changing to job rotations rather than practicing tenure, or a long possession of one office. Every politician in town worried about his job.

Rumors spread about like the flu, and everyone lived in fear of saying the wrong thing in front of the wrong person. In the end, the administration only replaced about one out of every 10 officials, or 10 for every 100.

> **Fast Fact:** *A president has a Cabinet made up of appointed leaders from each executive branch of the government. The Cabinet meets together weekly with the President to discuss important issues. The leaders include the Vice President and heads of Agriculture, Commerce, Defense, Education, Energy, Health and Human Services, Homeland Security, Housing and Urban Development, Interior, Labor, State, Transportation, Treasury, Veterans Affairs, and the Attorney General.*

The first Cabinet Jackson surrounded himself with was a room full of advisors who had defended him or helped him on the road to the White House. They included Martin Van Buren as Secretary of State. Van Buren had helped Jackson win New York votes. For Head of the Treasury, he chose Samuel Ingham, who had drummed up Pennsylvania support. Mr. John Brand from North Carolina became Secretary of the Navy, and his good friend from Tennessee, John Eaton, was assigned to serve as Secretary of War. Ignoring what anyone else thought about his choices, President Jackson made his own nephew a personal secretary.

The President's official Cabinet members weren't his only advisors. Jackson kept his closest friends within reach. They came and went freely to the White House to smoke, talk, and share ideas. Some say they walked in through the White House kitchens, and before long, the press officially named them "The Kitchen Cabinet."

Most of the Kitchen Cabinet members were newspaper men; some of them long, loyal friends Jackson could trust. Among them were Martin Van Buren, John Eaton, Robert Taney; newspaper editors Duff Green, Isaac Hill, Francis Blair, and Amos Kendall; and William Berkley Lewis who had served in the military under Jackson. Together, they were an intelligent, influential, and powerful group.

One of the first social scandals of Jackson's presidencies developed quickly after he made John Eaton Secretary of War. Eaton was a widower — a man who had already lost a wife — who fell in love with a younger family friend, Peggy O'Neal. Although she was also newly widowed, he married her before President Jackson's inauguration and brought her to Washington.

Peggy was said to be the most beautiful woman in Washington. It didn't help that gossip accused her of being a flirt, having a friendship with Eaton while she was married, and not grieving for her first husband after he died. The wives of the other women in the Cabinet refused to have anything to do with her, and the couple did not make the guest list to many parties.

President Jackson had seen women treat other women like this before. It had not been too long since Rachel had died, and he remembered the pain that criticism and gossip caused her. Unafraid to mix business with private problems, he defended Peggy Eaton publicly and demanded that his Cabinet advisors repair the situation both in public and at home with their wives.

No one would budge. The president quit attending Cabinet meetings. He turned to his Kitchen Cabinet for advice. As the scandal continued to grow, Jackson decided it was a bad image for the Democratic Party and asked the Cabinet to resign. The only advisor who stayed on was Martin Van Buren, and he was not married. Critics dubbed the whole disaster the Petticoat Affair.

The Cotton Tariff

President Jackson was so determined to do the will of the people that he made several landmark decisions. He felt Congress was still ruled by the upper class, so he used the power of veto with no apologies. He rejected bills so many times he passed up the number of vetoes made by all the presidents before him combined.

> **Fast Fact:** A veto is the power given to the President by the Constitution to cancel a bill sent by Congress so that it cannot become law.

As a young republic, America soon learned that taxes were necessary to help the government run. Although they fought for independence from England partly because they were taxed without representatives, taxes, or tariffs, were needed to build roads and feed armies.

In 1816, a decade before Jackson's presidency, a tariff charged a 20 to 25 percent tax on all goods brought in from other countries to be paid by those foreign countries. Before long, the Tariff of 1824 raised the tax penalty 10 percent higher. This tariff applied to iron, wool, cotton, and hemp.

Things got worse in 1828. Congress raised the tariff again, this time by 50 percent. Americans were outraged. They called it the Tariff of Abominations. The southern states were the angriest. The North was more industrialized and could produce its own iron, wool, cotton, and hemp faster and cheaper than their southern neighbors. They could charge what they wanted to the lower states. This meant the South would pay more if they bought from the North.

The tariff also meant the British would pay penalties if they tried to bring their own goods in to the South at a cheaper rate. A final blow was that the cost of cotton would go up in order to compensate for the taxes. This would make it harder for the Southern plantations to sell to anyone.

The cost of raw cotton grown in the Southern states went up, and England quit buying as much as they had before the new tariff. The Vice President, John C. Calhoun, came from South Carolina. The southern states demanded he do something about the unfair tax. He had to act to save his career, so he decided individual states should have the right to nullify, or even reverse, federal laws.

In 1832, Congress created a new bill that lowered the tariff, but not enough to help business in the South. In South Carolina, the State House decided to nullify the tariff altogether. They called their response the South Carolina Ordinance of Nullification and made it state law in November of the same year. In other words, they told the White House the tariff did not apply to the State of South Carolina.

This action created questions about state rights. Jackson knew it could become a reason for states to fight against other states. Worse, states could fight the federal government. The President went to Congress and complained that South Carolina had committee treason. He wrote a document called the Nullification Proclamation and asked permission for the White House to use federal troops to enforce federal laws that states refused to obey.

Today, many historians believe President Jackson's quick response to the divide over the federal tariff was a courageous act. They believe that a South Carolina nullification over one bill would have made it easier to ignore other laws. Ultimately, it could have caused a battle between federal and state troops.

The Power Struggle

The quality of transportation was improving, and the country needed to continue to build roads. In 1830, Congress decided it would be a good idea to invest in a company that would build part of a modern, national highway in Kentucky. The Maysville, Washington, Paris, and Lexington Turnpike Road Company wanted to build the road from Lexington, Kentucky to the Ohio River. They asked Congress to pay for it. Called the Maysfield Road Bill, the purchase would be for $50,000 worth of stock in the road building company.

Supporters of the bill argued that the road would be part of an interstate system that would connect Ohio all the way to Alabama. Though this part of the road would be entirely built in Kentucky, it would join a highway called the National Cumberland Road, which would link states together.

Enemies of the bill came mostly from the southern states. They felt like this bill gave the federal government too much power. Some said it infringed on their rights. Others didn't like the idea of Congress spending money just for the state of Kentucky.

Congress passed the bill, but the president rejected it by using his power of the veto. He said it wasn't constitutional, because the road would be in Kentucky. That meant it was a state business. Some critics felt his veto was personal, because he didn't get along with Henry Clay. Others said he was supporting Martin Van Buren's hope to keep the Erie Canal in New York a monopoly.

> In response, Jackson published this statement:
> *"It has no connection with any established system of improvements; is exclusively within the limits of a State, starting at a point on the Ohio River and running out 60 miles to an interior town, and even as far as the State is interested conferring partial instead of general advantages"* (History Engine, 2008–2015).

He also defended his decision based on the words in the Constitution. He felt Congress should only control money for the country as a whole, not state by state. He added the fact he was trying to pay off the national debt.

 Fast Fact: The four-mile Kentucky modern road Congress wanted to pay for would be 50 feet wide and have drainage ditches. This meant more traffic could pass with heavier loads than usual, and wet weather and mud would not be a problem.

While it's easy to understand why Jackson vetoed the bill, he had deeper concerns. America was still struggling to figure out how much power to give to states and how much power to allow the federal government in Washington.

In a letter to Congress, Jackson later explained to them that he felt the government should not invest in private companies. This could be dangerous, because unelected individuals from those companies would control the management of funds. They would have power over public money, and the voice of the people would have no importance. He told them he found this "inconceivable" and "dangerous." The President agreed with the South that building roads within a state should be taken care of at local levels.

The Indian Removal Act and The Trail of Tears

Although Jackson had defeated the Creeks and Seminoles, it didn't put an end to battles between settlers and Native Americans. One of the most controversial acts of the Presidency was the decision to deal with the constant clashes between Indians and Americans in the South. To make matters worse, gold was discovered in Cherokee territory in the state of Georgia. Governor George Gilmer complained to Washington that he had no authority to give rights or protection to the either the Cherokee or the trespassing miners. Something had to be done.

The people demanded action, and in May, Congress passed The Indian Removal Act. This law gave the federal government the right to meet with tribal chiefs for negotiations to move the tribes further west into territory that is a part of Oklahoma today. In reality, it demanded the Indians give up their homes and lands to the United States and pushed them out of the way.

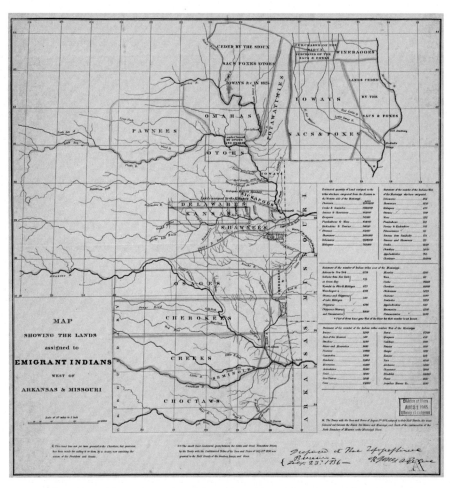

This map shows the approximate boundaries of the lands assigned to the relocated tribes in territories west of the Mississippi by 1836. The different colors represent the different tribes. This map also shows the southwestern border of the United States with Mexico, which at the time (the 1830s), was about to become the Independent Republic of Texas. (Map courtesy of Library of Congress)

A Virginia newspaper defended the law. It claimed that the Indians would not be forced to go and that they would be given money for expenses and their first year of life in the new land. In Washington, the President stated it would "separate the Indians from immediate contact with settlements of whites; [and] enable them to pursue happiness in their own way, and under their own crude institutions" (Globe, 1830).

Those who spoke out against The Indian Removal Act included Davy Crockett and Abraham Lincoln. It made no difference. President Andrew Jackson signed the Indian Removal Act on May 28, 1830. It gave him the right to grant the Indians lands in the West as a trade for the Union taking over the lands of their ancestors.

Although the Indians had the right to meet for negotiations, there would be little choice in the matter in the long run. They would have to move. The pressure to submit to the will of the Republic fell on the Indians. Many of the tribes hesitated. They saw no reason or right for them to be kicked off their lands. When the Indian fighter, Andrew Jackson, won the White House election again two years later, most of the leaders finally agreed to go.

The majority of the tribes went peacefully, but not all of them. They sent delegations and petitions to Washington. They even took their case to the Supreme Court. Loss after loss doing things the white man's way left many frustrated and depressed.

As a treaty was drawn up that gave the United States the right to take Indian lands in exchange for western territory, supplies, and money, a small group of Cherokee Indians received permission to meet with President Jackson in person. They called him the "Great Father." He had already met with some of their greatest lawyers and defenders but turned them away. The Indians must have felt this would be their last hope.

> Jackson was prepared with a stern and logical speech. It began: *"Brothers, I have long viewed your condition with great interest. For many years I have been acquainted with your people, and under all variety of circumstances, in peace and war. (...) You are now placed in the midst of a white population..."*

The president continued, telling the representatives they were now subject to the same laws and consequences of white settlers. He scolded them for their violence as well as growing problems with alcohol. They didn't do much to farm or modernize their lands the way whites thought it should be done. He warned them they would eventually disappear like the Indian nations before them if they didn't learn the white man's ways.

He eventually closed with what he considered wise counsel. "You have but one remedy within your reach. And that is to remove to the West and join your countrymen, who are already established there. The choice is yours. May the great spirit teach you how to choose."

 Fast Fact: The land of the Cherokee once covered 40,000 square miles with a population of about 26,000 people in the mid-1600s. Their nation included parts of Tennessee, Georgia, and North and South Carolina.

Eventually, the Cherokees submitted to a Senate-approved final treaty when it was sent to their own National Council in New Echota, Georgia. They were forced to surrender all of their lands east of the Mississippi for $5 million. Along with the new territory granted to them in the West, they would receive regular shipments of supplies like blankets, kettles, and rifles.

In the winter of 1838, the last of some stubborn Cherokee tribes were lined up and walked out by force. Thousands of them died along the way, earning the march the name The Trail of Tears.

The Battle of the Banks

The famous Bank Bill Veto of 1832 was the result of President Jackson's war on the Second Bank of the United States. Jackson did not trust banks or credit. He thought people shouldn't spend money they didn't really have. Promises and paper money were bad ideas. In his opinion, only gold and silver were the safe ways to do business, but there was no National Treasury building at that time to keep coins safe.

Jackson knew the First Bank of the Unites States had caused problems. He'd watched people lose homes and land in the Panic of 1819 when the Second Bank ran things badly, too.

 Fast Fact: Andrew Jackson once accepted paper promise payment for a land sale. When the buyer went bankrupt, the payment no longer had any value. This put the future president into so much debt he was almost ruined.

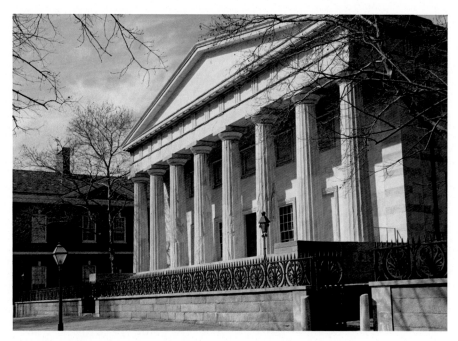

This image shows the Custom House, formerly the Second Bank of the United States, built in 1821-24 in Philadelphia. (Photo credit: Shutterstock.com)

After the War of 1812, the United States enjoyed economic growth and prospered. A second national bank was needed to give credit so Americans could continue buying land. Factories and roads could be built. A charter was approved in 1816, and the Second Bank of the United States was formed. The government owned 20 percent of it. Private investors controlled the rest.

The bank was run by a man name William Jones who had a bad record when it came to managing money. His poor management created the Panic of 1819 when the bank gave out more credit than it could afford to people who could not pay back their loans. It caused an economic depression for two years. This meant prices went up, people could not find jobs, and debtors were sent to prison. Many people lost everything.

In 1823, a wealthy Philadelphia man named Nicholas Biddle was chosen as a new president of the Second Bank. Biddle was a smart and successful businessman and politician. He was friends with other politicians like Henry Clay and John Calhoun. Being bank president made him a very powerful man.

The Second Bank had 25 branches, or offices, spread around the country. It competed with smaller state banks around the country that were operated by supporters of Jackson. About 40 members of Congress had stock in the national Second Bank, and many of them were enemies of the President.

Almost as soon as Andrew Jackson was elected, the bank wars began. It did not help that the president announced it would be his personal mission to destroy the bank, and that included never approving a new charter.

A bank needed to have a charter in order to operate, and the Second Bank of the United States had a charter that would expire in 1836. Supporters of the bank hoped by that time Jackson would no longer be president. They wanted him to be unpopular, so they decided to apply for a new charter ahead of time while he was still president. This fight was led by the bank president, Nicholas Biddle, his congressional friend and leader, Henry Clay, and other politicians who owned stock in the bank.

In 1832, the Second Bank requested that Congress renew their charter, and a bill was passed. As promised, the President used his powers of the veto to stop the plan. Back in Congress, his enemies rallied up enough votes to pass it anyway. After Jackson was re-elected in 1832, he made it one of the battle cries of his campaign. He reportedly told a group of bankers, "You are a den of vipers and thieves. I intend to rout you out, and by the eternal God, I will rout you out" (**www.ushistory.org**).

A year after his second election, President Jackson decided to find a way to remove money from the Second Bank until it could no longer function. At the time, the government had $9 million in the bank. Jackson ordered that no more money should be sent to the national bank. He took the money that was in it out, and he divided it between 89 smaller state banks run by his supporters and friends. Critics called them his "Pet Banks."

Henry Clay and other politicians were furious. They wanted to punish the President, so they convinced the Senate to censure, or publicly criticize, him. They demanded he provide them with documents showing he did not intend to defund the bank on purpose. He replied that criticizing a president was unconstitutional and ignored them.

Fast Fact: *The Second Bank of the United States went out of business in 1841.*

The battles created by the Bank Veto in 1832 had some positive effects. One of those was the government was able to pay off the National Debt. Eventually, there was a surplus of money. Banks were able to grow and prosper, and for a time, there was an economic boom.

There were problems that came with dissolving the Second Bank, too. States chartered risky banks out west called "Wildcat Banks" that dealt with land speculation. Some of the state banks that received money from the President begin to give out too much credit. These issues were dealt with by a Jackson order titled the "Specie Circular." He instructed banks to only accept gold or silver to avoid any problems.

In the end, President Jackson broke up the rich and powerful by taking apart the Second Bank of the United States. However, his actions also helped form a new political party, the Whigs, who opposed the Democrats. Later, the "Specie Circular" was blamed for another financial panic in 1837 that the new president, President Martin Van Buren, had to deal with.

Another Win

Four years after his first term as president, friends and supporters urged Jackson to run again in the 1832 election. Although not everyone liked him or his policy decisions, the majority of the people liked what he had accomplished. Many still saw him as an American hero. Even Democrats who disagreed with his controversial decisions stood behind him. They knew if they didn't support him, they would probably lose their jobs for punishment when he was re-elected.

The National Republican Party nominated Henry Clay. He finally mustered the courage to run against Old Hickory. He was still not a fan. Clay declared that Jackson was a "would-be tyrant" (Brands, 2005). Daniel Webster, a senator, expressed his concern that Jackson encouraged problems between the rich and poor. Critics of Jackson called him King Andrew. It was at this time that the Bank Wars broke out. Jackson's enemies hoped it would cost him the election.

The race was easy enough. President Jackson won the electoral votes 219 to 49. The popular vote came in at over 60 percent for Jackson and his new vice-president, Martin Van Buren. The country celebrated with parties and parades. One New York procession was over a mile long. There were pictures of President Jackson. Political banners, some showing eagles, were waved by enthusiastic democratic members.

The President went right back to business. There was no time to waste, because many of his scandals and controversies trickled right into the second term. The new political party, the Whigs, organized to fight against Jackson and his policies.

During this second term, Henry Clay led the charge to censure Jackson for his part in shutting down the Second Bank. It had little effect on the president's popularity, and eventually the whole business was removed from record. Everywhere he went, Jackson continued to be mobbed by crowds. Even up in the northern states where he toured to make peace with his enemies and those who didn't like his policies, people showed up by the thousands.

Whether Jackson traveled by horse or steamboat, people overwhelmed him. Sometimes, he stood outside for so long he would get sunburned. Other times, he'd shake so many hands his arm would hurt. In New York, a bridge collapsed under the weight of all of the spectators who had lined up to see him. So disgusted by this show of hero worship, the former president, John Quincy Adams, wrote that Jackson would "be glorified to the grave" (Brands, 2005).

Not all of the crowds were fans, though. Sometimes, Jackson's enemies showed up, and they came with weapons. In Virginia, he was assaulted by a sailor who slapped him in the face. In 1835, a man burst out of the crowd at the Capital just as the President was leaving. The man raised a pistol and shot at him — twice. Both times, the gun misfired.

Fast Fact: *The pistol that was fired at President Jackson was later tested. It shot perfectly fine, and the police could not explain why it had not worked the first two times.*

Jackson prepared to leave the White House in 1837 and return to Tennessee at last. It was just in time, because another financial panic loomed on the horizon and would affect the next president. His vice-president, Martin Van Buren, was elected and would carry on the Democratic cause.

There had been many changes in America, in politics, and at the White House, too. During Jackson's administration, he added the North Portico as it stands today. Inside, he installed iron pipes to draw water from a well to all parts of the house so servants wouldn't have to carry buckets anymore. A great deal of money was spent renovating public rooms. Andrew Jackson left his country and the presidential residence in good condition with a clear conscience. He had done his duty.

> 𝓙☞ **Fast Fact:** It takes 570 gallons of paint to paint the outside of the White House. Inside, there are 132 rooms and 35 bathrooms. There are 412 doors, 147 windows, 28 fireplaces, 8 staircases, and 3 elevators (**www.whitehouse.gov**).

Texas Independence

President Jackson always kept his eyes toward the West watching for opportunities to expand and protect his beloved republic. He had assumed Texas would be a part of the Louisiana Purchase, but in the end, President Adams gave it to the Spanish.

One of Jackson's important concerns when he was first elected president was to test Mexico to see if she was interested in selling Texas, or if there was a crafty way to win the territory without a war. He was the second president to offer to buy the territory but was not successful. The $1

Sam Houston (1793–1863)
(Photo credit: Shutterstock.com)

million was not enough for his representative to even offer once the man arrived to Mexico's capital. That left Jackson only one other choice.

Texas was governed poorly by the Mexicans, which worried the President. He felt France or England could barge in and take over at any time. He also didn't like the idea of Texas being settled by Americans and then becoming independent by not joining the United States. Last, most of the settlements of Texas were American and very close to Louisiana. With the help of at least two of his allies, Colonel Anthony Butler and Sam Houston, he eventually made his dreams of Texas come true.

By the time Jackson was in office, Spain had lost control of Texas and Mexico when the Mexicans won their independence in 1829. Before that time, in 1820, an American colonist, Stephen Austin, received permission from the Spanish government to bring hundreds of American families to the new region to help settle the land. The soil was good for farming cotton, and new slave laws were not enforced.

The American colonists were allowed to settle in Texas if they agreed to do three things: be loyal to Mexico, learn Spanish, and become Roman Catholic. Soon there were more Americans in the territory called *Tejas* than there were Mexicans. Before long, the Americans didn't like Spanish government. They wanted their own constitution, too.

The first thing President Jackson did was send a representative to Mexico City. He chose an army colonel named Anthony Butler. He phrased his desire to buy Texas as just a wish to pay some money to realign the current borders. Butler did his best but was overwhelmed by the amount of corruption by Mexican officials. He wrote the President that the only way to purchase Texas would be through bribery. Jackson refused on the grounds of personal and national honor.

In 1829, the military hero known as General Antonio López de Santa Anna fought off Spain and retained Mexican independence. He not only became a hero, he came to power over the country by 1833. During this time, Jackson had been working with another very close friend on the Texas problem — Sam Houston.

Sam Houston had survived some tough years. He'd left his position as governor of Tennessee over a marriage scandal. He struggled with alcohol. Congress charged him for beating a congressman on Pennsylvania Avenue with a cane after the man criticized him on the floor of the House. All Houston wanted to do was find peace in the land of Texas, but he knew it would need independence from Mexico for Americans to be safe there.

Mexico was very suspicious of Colonel Butler and the United States. It didn't look like a deal would be possible. Jackson decided to send down Houston as General Sam Houston the Indian Agent. Houston's official job was to take care of Indian problems in Texas, but he was really there to report back to Jackson what was going on with the Mexican government. The President wanted to know how much control they had over the territory.

Houston told Jackson that the people of Texas pretty much did what they wanted. They brought in slaves illegally and ignored many of the Mexican laws. He told the president that Mexico was "powerless" and "penniless" to do anything about them. They were in the middle of a civil war. To make matters worse, Creek Indians were settling on the American side of the borders.

 Fast Fact: Following in the footsteps of many other nations, Mexico abolished slavery in 1831. This meant a loss of manpower for plantations and farms that used slave labor. It was a problem that affected the plans of new Texas colonists. England abolished the practice in 1838. The United States did not abolish slavery until 1865.

Like he originally suspected, Jackson knew it would only be a matter of time before another nation came in and took over. It was just a question of who could grab up Texas first.

In 1835, the Americans decided they had put up with enough. They gathered together to fight for Texas independence from Mexico. Sam Houston was made general over the Texas Army. After a few small battles, they captured San Antonio and declared themselves the winners. President Jackson pretended to have nothing to do with it. He insisted the United States government was neutral. This did not satisfy everyone in Washington, though. Many feared Texas would become another Southern state and join the South in fighting over the slavery issue.

General Santa Anna was now running Mexico. He was furious with America. He warned Jackson if he became involved with the Americans claiming Texas as an independent republic, he would march in and burn Washington to ashes. The President could not encourage Texas to join the United States. He couldn't even recognize their independence without Congress.

Who was General Santa Anna? General Antonio López de Santa Anna was born in the Mexican state called Veracruz. He joined the military at only 15 years old and fought for independence from Spain. He next became active in politics, learning how to take down his enemies through power and manipulation. After he fought off Spain again in 1828, he became the popular hero that would protect Mexico and all of its territories. He had no intention of allowing Texas to become an independent nation.

After Houston and his forces took control of San Antonio and other towns, Santa Anna arrived in 1835, and the famous Texas Revolution began its brief and bloody struggle. Santa Anna won back the Alamo in

San Antonio and executed the famous and beloved Davy Crockett. A year later, Sam Houston met him at the Battle of San Jacinto with around only 900 volunteers.

The winning battle against General Santa Anna happened as a surprise attack on the San Jacinto River. Houston had received news the Mexican army would have to cross a bridge to return back from chasing colonists, and so he waited.

While the Mexicans were resting, about 3:30 in the late afternoon, Houston ordered the attack. The Texans launched cannon fire, shot guns, and used hand-to-hand combat against the surprised troops to win the battle in a matter of 20 minutes. Over 600 Mexicans were killed in a violent slaughter that Houston reportedly tried to stop. The Texans only lost nine men.

Although he mysteriously disappeared after the battle, Santa Anna was captured the next day wearing regular soldiers' clothing and hiding in tall grass. Houston wanted to execute him, but President Jackson warned him of the consequences of looking like a tyrant. He had learned his own lesson about not acting with government approval in Florida.

Houston sent Santa Anna to Jackson in Washington instead. The President offered the military general and Mexican President $3.5 million dollars in exchange for Texas and California, plus a ride back to Mexico City aboard a U.S. Navy ship.

> **Fast Fact:** *General Santa Anna fought the French and others in battles over the next 15 years. He lost a leg, which helped his popularity, but he struggled to stay in power. In 1853, the United States bought up more Mexican territory, and he lost what was left of his support. The once famous military conqueror died a poor man 23 years later.*

President Jackson did not recognize Texas as independent until his last day in office. Afterward, it took years before the republic was admitted to the United States. Many did not want Texas to join, because it would upset the balance of states fighting over slavery. There was a great deal of fighting in the government and the newspapers.

After Jackson left office, President Van Buren wouldn't come to a decision, and nothing happened. From Tennessee, Jackson did not shy away from expressing his disappointments and frustrations. When James K. Polk promised to annex Texas if he won the 1844 election, Jackson was excited and happy to support him.

President Polk was determined, but he never had the chance. The outgoing president beat him to it. The resolution to accept Texas to the Union was signed on March 1, 1845, just before the tenth president, John Tyler, left office.

" Jackson was thrilled with the news. It didn't matter to him who did it. *"I ... congratulate my beloved country [that] Texas is reannexed,"* he wrote, *"and the safety, prosperity, and the greatest interest of the whole Union is secured by this...great and important national act"* (Remini, 1986).

Chapter Nine: The Jacksonian Legacy

President Andrew Jackson died on June 8, 1845, eight years after he left the White House in the hands of his former vice-president and successor, Martin Van Buren. He was satisfied with his replacement and wrote him regularly up until his death.

In President Jackson's farewell address, he spoke words of gratitude directly to the people of his country. He told them being president put him in difficult situations. He also explained that sometimes decisions had to be made very fast. Jackson promised the people that he always tried to do what was best for America, and he thanked them for understanding and supporting him.

The President also declared that democracy was no longer an experiment, because the Union had succeeded. "…[O]ur country has improved and is flourishing beyond any former example in the history of nations." On the other hand, although he was proud of the Union, he warned that the North and South had to come together on the slavery issue. He worried the strong feelings could continue to create problems that could lead to serious consequences. "What have you to gain by division and dissension?" he asked the country.

Before finishing his speech, President Jackson made several remarks about the banking problems in the country and his concerns over the struggling financial system. In his final words, he acknowledged his old age and illnesses, his love for his country, and finally, "I bid you a last and affectionate farewell."

The President returned home to the Hermitage and the beloved grave of his departed Rachel.

> 🖐☞ **Fast Fact:** *You can read President Jackson's actual farewell address in its entirety online at The American Presidency Project* (**www.presidency.ucsb.edu/ws/?pid=67087**).

Life had gone on at the Hermitage under the direction of overseers that were hired and fired, much like Jackson's advisors in Washington. When he arrived home, he found there were more horses and other farm animals than could be properly cared for. The slaves on his land numbered about 150, and problems with them plagued him for years. Debt stacked up, and money shortages soon became such a problem that he had to refuse an invitation to visit the anniversary celebration of the Battle of New Orleans.

Things weren't going so well for the country, either. Some of the Cherokee and Seminoles who had refused to leave under Jackson's treaty had dug in their heels and were fighting the new presidential administration. The abolitionists, those who wanted to end slavery, had the country in turmoil. Even the economy took a turn. The banking system verged on another financial collapse, and his old banking enemy, Nicholas Biddle, loudly blamed Andrew Jackson for all of the problems.

Jackson ignored the political blame game and made no comments to the papers. He began to sell off some of his land and horses to make ends meet. His son, Andrew Jackson Junior, also had money problems, which led Jackson to request a $6,000 loan to satisfy both of their debts.

Age and illness began to take a serious toll. The president's death was a slow and painful journey. From as early as the 1820s, he had become more committed to his religion. He showed great respect to clergymen as well as his wife and mother. At times, he would be so ill with his usual symptoms that he could not walk or even write, but he appeared to have a confident and clear conscience.

Along the way, there were days when he felt quite well. He told one friend it seemed he went "in and out" like a candle. He celebrated the election of James K. Polk in 1845 as his health began to fade at a steady pace. Soon, he could not walk and could barely eat. His kidneys shut down. He slept a great deal.

Two weeks before his death, he hoped to make it to a meeting in the church he built for Rachel on the Hermitage property, but he was too sick. The minister visited him afterward, bringing him communion. Jackson took his children each by the hand and blessed them. He promised them his suffering was nothing compared to that of "his Savior." He then faded back into sleep on and off again. During most of the time he was awake, he prayed.

On Saturday, June 7, he felt cold and clammy, and he fainted. The family thought he had died and tried to move him, but he woke back up. He firmly asked to see his grandchildren once more. When they came to him, he gave them religious instruction and then asked for his glasses. After he could clearly see, he told those present he hoped to see them again in heaven, both black and white.

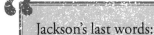

> Jackson's last words:
> *"Oh, do not cry — be good children & we will all meet in heaven"* (Remini, 1980).

The seventh president of the United States passed away at six in the evening. He was buried two days later beside his wife. At his funeral service, the seventh chapter of Revelation and 90th Psalms from the Bible was read. The mourners sang the great spiritual, *How Firm a Foundation*. The departing wishes of his friends and family were that he would be counted among the elect.

Controversies

Andrew Jackson always seemed to find himself in trouble whether he was a young boy, lawyer, military general, or even president. Because he was President of the United States, his controversies were known about all over the world.

When he vetoed the Mayfield Road Bill, Jackson defended the actual intentions of the Constitution. By refusing to become involved in Georgia's problems with the Indians, he supported state rights to legislate. Threatening South Carolina with war if they tried to nullify tax laws showed he would support the federal branch of the government in any way he had to do it.

The Andrew Jackson Monument in Jackson Square in New Orleans.
(Photo credit: Photospin.com)

Many of Jackson's issues that he had to deal with continued to be serious problems after he left the White House. His choices required a great deal of confidence and determination. Because of this, they followed him throughout history.

133

Slavery and Racism

Slavery is as controversial a subject now as it was 250 years ago. It is still a stain on the world today. A few years ago, the U.S. State Department reported that "only around 40,000 victims have been identified in the last year. In contrast, social scientists estimate that as many as 27 million men, women, and children are trafficking victims at any given time" (Trafficking in Persons, 2013).

It is a problem as old as time. In the new world, slaves were brought to the Caribbean and part of South America. They could be African, Irish, English, or European indentured servants. In early America, the Dutch brought the first African slaves in 1619. Over the next 100 years, numbers estimate that about 7 million African slaves were brought ashore.

 Fast Fact: England has been involved in slavery for over 2,000 years. The Romans enslaved Britons as early as 54 B.C. Later, the Irish slave trade began when 30,000 Irish prisoners were sent as slaves to the New World. In 1625, King James I sent more Irish as political prisoners to be sold to English settlers in the West Indies. Ireland became the source of slavery for English merchants until the later trade of African slaves.

Before cotton was the prize crop of the Southern states during Andrew Jackson's life, slaves worked in tobacco and rice fields. After the American Revolution, whites in the northern states felt like slavery was too similar to how they had been treated by England.

The issue was confusing, because the Constitution declared that all men were created equal. However, it also guaranteed the right to "repossess any person held to service or labor." Because there were both slave owners and men against it writing the Constitution, compromises were made. A great deal of the language was cloudy and left open one's own personal understanding.

About one-third of the people living in the Southern states were slaves. They were owned by masters of plantations and farms and had to live by their rules. Most slaves were not allowed to read or write. Families were separated. Many white masters had children with slave women. Any slaves that tried to rebel or run away were tortured as punishment and were sometimes killed.

Before the Civil War, there were a few slave revolts that succeeded in killing white slave owners, but they were quickly captured by locals and militia. These riots made rules and laws stricter in the southern states, but it strengthened the resolve of abolitionist in the North.

Andrew Jackson was like many plantation owners in the South. He opposed abolition, or ending slavery. Like Jackson, the southern states depended on slavery to produce what was grown and exported. The President also felt that slavery should be a state matter, not a federal one.

Slavery was an issue that raised guilty questions to men in the South, like Jackson, who considered themselves religious. Many slave masters thought of themselves as father figures. To avoid using the word "slave," they would use the word "servant." They also called their slaves their "boys and girls" or their "men."

As many northern states required that slavery end, congress outlawed the importation of slaves into the United States. That meant Africans could no longer be brought to America to be sold. Despite that, buying and selling slaves continued between slave owners inside the country. Jackson was still trading slaves at least as late as 1811. One record shows he paid up to $929 for new slaves.

By the time Jackson was in presidential politics, he had to deal with bad press from his critics because he was a slave owner. Most of the hard work required to build the Hermitage was done by slaves. His crops were grown and harvested the same way.

As an owner of enslaved people, Jackson believed in being strict but also providing the necessities. He would punish slaves if they ran away. He once advertised $50 for the return of a runaway. In 1827, one of his slaves, whom he called Gilbert, fought against a whipping after escaping a third time. He was killed by a supervisor, but Jackson was still held accountable for the death, especially by Northern political enemies.

As the issue became a big political problem in Washington, enemies like John Quincy Adams took the position that slavery itself would divide and destroy the Union. President Jackson saw it as a secession problem. He worried slavery would become an excuse for states to withdraw from the Union and possibly start a civil war. In the end, Jackson was right.

Many people feel Andrew Jackson was racist because of his attitudes toward Native Americans and enslaved people. While he never made public statements that revealed whether his heart felt it was right or wrong, he clearly was a slave owner and fought against policies that would set them free.

> Strangely, he felt comfortable calling on free men of color to fight for him and "their country" like he did at the Battle of New Orleans:
> *"To the Free Colored Inhabitants of Louisiana*
> *Through a mistaken policy, you have heretofore been deprived*
> *of a participation in the glorious struggle for national rights in*
> *which our country is engaged. This no longer shall exist.*
>
> *As sons of freedom, you are now called upon to defend our most*
> *inestimable blessing. As Americans, your country looks with*
> *confidence to her adopted children for a valorous support, as a*
> *faithful return for the advantages enjoyed under her mild and*
> *equitable government. As fathers, husbands, and brothers, you are*
> *summoned to rally around the standard of the Eagle, to defend all*
> *which is dear in existence..."*
>
> *(To the Men of Color, 1814).*

When it came to the Indians, Jackson made his feelings very clear. He called them savage and barbaric. According to him, their governments were "crude institutions." The well-respected Andrew Jackson historian, Robert V. Remini, wrote that "Jackson believed that Indians belonged to a lower order of humanity and that the federal government had the right to deal with them as it saw fit" (Remini, 2002).

Defenders of Andrew Jackson believe his Indian policies were a way to protect both settlers and Indians. The settlers did not respect Indian ways or rights, and they broke agreements that often led to wars. The Indians were in the way of settlers who were needed to expand America's boundaries. The President felt removing Indians far out of the way would preserve their culture and lives, and protect American citizens.

The Trail of Tears

President Jackson's Indian Removal Act had many opponents. His belief that the United States had the right to take land in order to grow replaced any fairness on the account of Native Americans.

In 1838, after he left the White House, the forced migration of remaining Cherokee Indians departed late in the year during rain and snow. Thousands of Indians died due to weather, illness, and starvation. This horrible event probably influenced the second Seminole Indian War when the United States tried to repeat it.

The Cherokee endured for many years after having most of their lands stolen from them, because they made great efforts to counsel with the country's leaders. They understood the importance of educating themselves and finding representation. Their people did not surrender without a legal fight. They had their own language, constitution, and schools. Some of them learned to farm and take advantage of white modern conveniences. Their leaders could read and write. Some of them were highly educated.

Leading up to the terrible Trail of Tears and ultimate Indian surrender, Cherokee leaders petitioned Congress to interfere in Georgia's new laws they found unfair. Their request for help from President Jackson was rejected. Finally, they decided to take their cause to the Supreme Court.

William Wirt represented the Cherokee Nation in the lawsuit. He demanded the United States force Georgia to allow the Cherokee to remain on their Georgia lands, because they had formed as an independent nation. The chief judge decided that the Cherokee were not an independent nation, but he sided with them when he agreed they were not subject to Georgia's state laws. The Indians thought they had won.

The United States disagreed. The state of Georgia pressured them to go. Tensions between settlers and natives continued. A Christian missionary newspaper declared that if "whites would not molest them," there wouldn't be any problems.

The Principle Chief of the Cherokee was a mixed blooded white man name John Ross. He was wealthy, educated, and refused to quit fighting for his people. He encouraged the Indians to be strong and determined. Leaders that went to Washington to argue came back beaten. Despite John Ross and his backing, a Treaty Party was formed to go to Washington to surrender and fight for the best agreement possible. They were later murdered; some in front of their own families.

John Ross would not surrender. He decided to go to Washington himself. He had fought with Andrew Jackson at the Battle of Horseshoe Bend. He hoped that this would help him win his argument that the Oklahoma region where the Cherokee would be forced to live was too badly watered and did not have enough forests.

The currently proposed treaty would allow white men to govern and regulate the Indian government on Indian lands. Knowing Jackson didn't help Ross after all. The President didn't like him. He did not consider Ross a real Indian, because he was only one-eighth Cherokee. He called him a half-breed and denied Ross had any real authority just because he was a Cherokee chief.

After several requests, the President did agree to meet with John Ross after all. He was surprised when the chief demanded the Cherokee be allowed to keep land already settled by whites in Tennessee, Georgia, and Alabama. Ross also demanded federal protection on their old lands for five years.

Jackson told him the only treaty would be one where all of the Cherokee people gave up all of their lands east of the Mississippi. Ross reminded him about the gold discovered on their land in Georgia and asked for $20 million in exchange for all of their lands and the gold. Instead of agreeing, old Sharp Knife became angry.

The President threatened Ross there would no longer be discussions if he continued to ask for ridiculous allowances. Ross was offered the $5 million, but he refused it and left Washington furious and defeated. The President later met to finalize the treaty with other Cherokee chiefs. It was then he reminded them they had no choice.

Some 2,000 Cherokees resigned themselves to the inevitable, packed their belongings, and headed west. Not everyone left immediately, though. John Ross continued to encourage his people to have hope and resist the change.

After President Jackson left the White House, the Cherokee had two years before their time was up. Later, President Van Buren was forced to officially order them to leave for Oklahoma or face military action.

The Trail of Tears began.

> 🖐☞ **Fast Fact:** The Trail of Tears is officially marked and recognized as being 2,200 miles long. It goes through nine states: Alabama, Arkansas, Georgia, Illinois, Kentucky, Missouri, North Carolina, Oklahoma, and Tennessee.

The Indians were attacked by federal troops in their homes. About 17,000 people were rounded up with no time to pack or prepare, and they were put in prisons until it was time to march west. Their homes and belongings were burned as they were led away. One witness confessed: "I fought through the Civil War and have seen men shot to pieces and slaughtered by thousands, but the Cherokee removal was the cruelest I ever saw" (Remini, 2001).

During their imprisonment before being led to Oklahoma, many Indians became sick and died. They were finally allowed to travel by boat and then put on to trains. It was hot, crowded, and there was not much food. On the journey, they were robbed or cheated by anyone with authority. Those who didn't die along the way were forced to walk the final miles to their new home. Historians estimate about 8,000 of the Cherokee died on the Trail of Tears — almost half of their people.

One general involved in the migration, Winfield Scott, admitted he worried the militia would be remembered as being cruel and "inhumane." Witnesses saw the starving Indians dying. Someone recorded, "these poor people were made the instruments of enriching a few unprincipled and wicked contractors" (Remini, 2001).

The blame for this great tragedy was placed at the feet of Andrew Jackson. Although he wasn't president went it happened, it was his policies that demanded Indians be removed from lands that would expand the United States. Some historians say that he wrote the next president about it and insisted that the government follow through and give no more time or allow any more excuses. Van Buren promised him the Indians would be forced out once and for all.

Others choose to blame Principle Chief John Ross. They feel if he would not have encouraged his people to fight or ignore the government, they wouldn't have stayed so long. Ross knew there would be no more talks, agreements, or help. Even though the Cherokee were out of time and luck, his decision not to surrender led to the high numbers of deaths.

> 👉 **Fast Fact:** Approximately 1,000 Cherokees escaped the government round up and avoided being forced to walk The Trail of Tears. In 1868, they established their own government in Cherokee, North Carolina, recognized by the United States. They are called the Eastern Band of Cherokee Indians and still live there today.

In the end, Andrew Jackson was right about one thing. He told the Cherokee that their people and way of life would be lost forever if they didn't move to Oklahoma. Despite the large number of deaths on the Trail of Tears, the Cherokee and their culture did survive whereas many other Southern tribes became extinct.

The Nullification Proclamation

When the Cotton Tariff that doubled taxes passed in 1828 and South Carolina rebelled, they created the South Carolina Ordinance of Nullification to fight back. Because President Jackson ultimately had to warn the state he would bring in federal troops, he made federal power quite controversial.

When the Cotton Tariff passed, the politicians in southern America who felt strongest about state rights began campaigning to nullify, or reverse, the law. Those for fighting the Cotton Tariff were called "nullies." They campaigned against the Cotton Tariff by using the state resolutions of Kentucky and Virginia, because they strongly supported state laws. They also claimed the Constitution allowed federal laws to be nullified.

Other states complained but did not support them. In the state legislature, there was some Unionist opposition to the nullies who felt they were wrong and the bill was blocked the first time.

One shocking supporter of South Carolina during this crisis was Vice President John C. Calhoun. He wrote a booklet for the state that argued that the Cotton Tariff was unconstitutional. The writings were anonymous when they were published, but it wasn't long before the country knew the Vice President would not side with President Jackson on this policy.

President Jackson was furious with Calhoun. They avoided each other so often that state dinners were tense and uncomfortable when they were both in the room. The Vice President hoped to be the next president, but along with other differences he had with Jackson, supporting South Carolina's attempts at federal nullification ruined his chances.

The nullification went to the legislature a second time, and this time, Unionists couldn't stop it. The South Carolina Ordinance of Nullification became law on November 24, 1832. This meant they would not recognize or obey the Cotton Tariff. Flags flew at half-mast. A new South Carolina governor was elected, and the state threatened Jackson they would leave the Union if the Cotton Tariff wasn't lifted.

King Andrew the First
(Photo courtesy of Library of Congress)

The President responded by ordering troops to South Carolina. When he spoke to Congress in December of 1832, he promised he would carry out his threats, but he did suggest they lower the tariff rates to meet the nullies halfway.

A week later, Jackson published the famous and controversial Nullification Proclamation that claimed states didn't have the right to abolish federal laws. He warned South Carolina about the dangers of fighting federal laws and asked Congress to create a Force Bill. They supported the President and authorized him to use military force against states to enforce federal law. The Nullification Proclamation became one of Jackson's biggest controversies.

> *Fast Fact:* Critics did not like the Force Bill, which gave the federal government the right to use military power against a state. Many people called it the Bloody Bill. When South Carolina canceled its nullification bills to avoid war, it nullified the Bloody Bill, too. The Nullification Proclamation and its Force, or Bloody, Bill came to be evidence used against Jackson that he was a power hungry dictator and military tyrant.

Rather than see a war, Vice President Calhoun went to Henry Clay and asked him to urge Congress to lower tax rates. The new plan lowered the tariff 10 percent over a period of eight years. Finally, the President and South Carolina came to an agreement, and a catastrophe was avoided.

History Remembers

History can't seem to decide if Andrew Jackson was a hero or dictator. Some of his names, like Old Hickory and Sharp Knife, are compliments.

Others, like King Andrew or The Napoleon of the Woods, show how some people felt he was a dictator.

Because of his bad temper and behavior as a young man, Jackson is often remembered as being an angry man with no self-control. He held grudges and used revenge. It didn't help that he had so many duels, either!

As a military general, some people believe he broke laws making his own decisions about when, who, and how to lead. Although he believed in serving his country first and upholding the Constitution, he didn't have a problem making unpopular or harsh choices if he felt the other alternative would harm the country.

As president, Jackson's Indian and slavery policies showed he felt America and the white man were more important than people of other colors. He is accused of having "violent hatreds" toward those who were different or didn't agree with him. Today, he is sometimes called a tyrant, racist, or the "American Caesar."

Others feel President Jackson was a true patriot and American hero. He never used the tragedies or sicknesses in his life as excuses not to do his duty or serve the people. He loved and treated his wife and family with respect and honor. If he felt something was right, he would say it or do it even if it was unpopular. That took great bravery.

Fans of Andrew Jackson believe he is a symbol of the American Dream and what anyone can accomplish if they work hard enough. They believe he is the best example of a true democrat and individualist.

Andrew Jackson in the 21st Century

The seventh president of the United States made a mark in American History that affected how we have grown geographically and developed politically. By entering into politics and standing up for what he believed was best for the Union, he created the Democratic Party. His enemies were inspired to organize as Whigs in order to defeat him. This created the national two-party system we have today.

> 👉 *Fast Fact:* President Andrew Jackson's image was printed on the $20 bill in 1928. In 2016, Treasury Secretary Jacob J. Lew proposed that Jackson be replaced with the face of an African American slave and abolitionist, Harriet Tubman.

As the President, Jackson led by fierce example how to deal with trouble in Congress. He did not force legislation upon the people, but used his power of the veto to stop lawmakers from taking advantage of American citizens. During his career, he vetoed 12 bills.

President Jackson was a man of the people. He spoke to America when he spoke to Congress. He listened and tried to represent the people over other politicians. As president, he shaped our future banking and financial system. As a military leader, his service helped the United States secure Florida, Louisiana, and Texas.

When he left the office of president and returned home to the Hermitage, Jackson was as famous as he'd ever been. Before he was elected, people still argued about whether or not democracy would work. After his administration, the country knew that the checks and balances of elected representatives in Congress and a President in the White House made the country safe from tyranny.

Andrew Jackson was one of the first American leaders to live the American Dream. His parents were poor immigrants, and his beginnings were humble and hard. He went from life in a frontier log cabin to the courtrooms of a lawyer and judge. He married his true love and built his home in the hills of Tennessee. As a senator, he served the people of his state. He fought for Westward expansion as a general, and he became the President of the United States.

No matter how he is remembered, he served his people up until his death with courage, confidence, and fiery determination.

(Photo credit: Photospin.com)

Author's Note

A couple of hours away from the hectic streets of Atlanta where I live rests a quiet stretch of meadow and trees broken up by a lazy, winding river. Here in Daviston, Alabama, lies the National Military Park of Horseshoe Bend where Americans defeated the Creek Indians under the leadership of Andrew Jackson. It's so peaceful now it's hard to believe two centuries ago the air echoed with cannon fire, drum beats, and musket shots. It's hard to understand why a man would fight another to the death because of his traditions and the color of his skin.

History is not boring. It always has an interesting, exciting, or important story to tell. When we look behind us, we can find mistakes that need correction or discover great examples of courage in the most terrible of circumstances. History teaches us that heroes are not chosen; they are made. And they choose to be made.

As of today, President Andrew Jackson has not escaped his controversies from over 200 years ago. Despite his heroic stand against the British in New Orleans, his legacy is stained with ties to racism and the presidential misuse of power. Did he have his reasons? An important thing we can learn by diving into American History is that there are smaller, lesser-known details that influenced the choices of our leaders whether we agree with them or not.

As a researcher and author, the most striking thing I realized about Andrew Jackson was that he loved his family and country above all else. I admire his courage and strength, and yet I often find myself shaking my head at his dangerous temper and pride. Whew! Despite his weaknesses and a few serious mistakes, this tale of Old Hickory has made me believe that in his heart, he felt he was a man of honor. Andrew Jackson lived his life doing what he believed was truly the right thing to do. That is a great message.

A special thank you to Atlantic Publishing for giving me the opportunity to write about real men and women who helped shape the America we have today. Thank you to my editor, Rebekah Sack, for editing pages of fascinating Andrew Jackson stories I scrawled out and for helping them make sense for readers. A writer cannot write without the cooperation and understanding of family and friends, so props to my loved ones. Last, a special acknowledgment to modern historian and biographer, H.W. Brands, for his excellent volume on President Jackson with sources and citations that led me on great adventures through the Library of Congress.

I encourage you, dear reader, to keep reading and studying the heroes and villains of the past. There are wonderful books and resources today that provide actual documents which allow us to hear in their own words the hopes, dreams, and ideas of the men and women that shaped this country — and the world — for you and me.

— Danielle Thorne

1767:   Andrew Jackson is born in South Carolina.
        Rachel Donelson is born in Halifax County, Virginia.
1775:   The American Revolution costs the first American blood at the
        Battle of Lexington.
1776:   The Declaration of Independence is signed in Philadelphia,
        Pennsylvania.
1783:   The American Revolution ends at the Battle of Yorktown in
        Virginia.
1787:   Andrew Jackson receives his law degree in North Carolina.
1788:   Andrew Jackson arrives in Nashville.
        Andrew Jackson receives his first slave as payment for services
        rendered.
1791:   Andrew Jackson marries Rachel Donelson in Natchez in the
        Mississippi Territory.
1793:   The Cherokee Indians attack Knoxville.
        Sam Houston is born in Virginia.
1796:   The Jacksons buy Hunters Hill in Nashville.
        Andrew Jackson serves as a delegate in the Knoxville Convention.
        Tennessee becomes a state.

1798:   Andrew Jackson is elected as Senator of Tennessee.

1802:   Andrew Jackson is elected Major General of the Militia of Tennessee.

1804:   The Jacksons buy the land for the Nashville Hermitage.

1806:   Andrew Jackson kills Charles Dickinson in a famous duel.

1807:   The British fire on the *USS Chesapeake*.

1808:   The United States makes it illegal to import slaves.

1809:   The Jacksons adopt their nephew, Andrew Jackson Junior.

1812:   The War of 1812 between the British and United States begins over differences.

1813:   Andrew Jackson is shot twice in a fight at the Nashville Inn.
         The Creek Indian Wars begin in Alabama.
         The Fort Mims Massacre near Mobile costs hundreds of settlers their lives.
         Andrew Jackson defeats the Creeks at the Battle of Horseshoe Bend.

1814:   The Treaty of Fort Jackson ends the Creek Wars.

1815:   The Battle of New Orleans is led by Andrew Jackson against a British invasion.
         The Treaty of Ghent ends the War of 1812.

1816:   A charter is issued for the Second Bank of the United States of America.
         Andrew Jackson fights the Florida Seminoles.
         Andrew Jackson captures Florida territory from the British.

1819:   The Spanish officially surrender Florida to the United States.
         The Financial Panic of 1819 ruins many families.

1820:   Stephen Austin and his group of American colonists settle parts of Texas with permission from the Spanish government.
         The Pirate Lafitte flees Texas waters after his service in The Battle of New Orleans and disappears somewhere in South America.

1821:   Mexico wins independence from Spain.

1823:   Nicholas Biddle becomes President of the Second Bank of the United States of America.

1824:   Pennsylvania nominates Andrew Jackson as a presidential candidate.

Andrew Jackson runs for seventh President of the United States and loses.

The Tariff of 1824 is passed.

1828:   Andrew Jackson is elected President of the United States.

Rachel Donelson Jackson dies.

The controversial Cotton Tariff is passed.

1830:   The Maysfield Road Act is passed in Congress but is vetoed by Andrew Jackson.

The Indian Removal Act is passed.

1831:   Mexico abolishes slavery in 1829. It becomes official two years later for all of Mexico and its territories, which make up most of the southwestern United States today.

1832:   Andrew Jackson is re-elected for a second term as President of the United States.

The Second Bank of the United States asks Congress to renew its charter.

The Bank Bill Veto gives the President power to change the banking system.

The South Carolina Ordinance of Nullification is passed by South Carolina to ignore federal law.

The Nullification Proclamation and Force Bill give the President power to send federal troops into states that challenge federal law.

1833:   General Santa Ana comes to power in Mexico.

1835:   The Texas Revolution begins, and Sam Houston leads the charge.

1837:   Andrew Jackson leaves the White House and returns to The
        Hermitage.
        Martin Van Buren is elected eighth President of the United States.
        The Financial Panic of 1837 creates a crisis that lasts for several
        years.

1838:   The Cherokee walk the Trail of Tears.
        The Battle of the Alamo is lost to General Santa Ana, and Davy
        Crockett is executed.
        England abolishes slavery.

1841:   The Second Bank of the United States of America goes out of
        business.

1845:   The death of Andrew Jackson is mourned across the country.
        James K. Polk is elected 11th President of the United States.
        Texas is admitted to the Union.

Glossary

abolitionists: protesters or opponents of slavery.

acre: an area of land that equals 4,840 square yards.

administration: the governing time period of a specific president.

Alamo: a small building in San Antonio, Texas, built in the 18ᵗʰ century as a Roman Catholic mission and fortress.

American Caesar: a nickname for Andrew Jackson that referred to Caesar, a historical Roman dictator.

American Dream: the idea that everyone has the equal right to opportunity and success no matter who they are or where they come from.

aristocrat: a person with noble or royal blood.

Bank Bill Veto of 1832: President Andrew Jackson's veto of the bill for the new charter for the Second Bank of the United States.

Battle of Horseshoe Bend: the final bloody battle of the Creek Wars between General Andrew Jackson and the Red Stick Creek Indians in southeast Alabama.

bayou: a marshy, still channel of water common in Louisiana.

blackleg: a swindler; someone who tricks or cheats.

block (blockade): when military forces guard or block a position so that the enemy cannot pass.

Bloody Bill: another name for the **Force Bill.**

boarders: a lodger or renter who is provided with meals.

branches: a smaller division of a business.

cabinet: advisors to the President of the United States who are the heads of executive departments.

caucus: a meeting of political party members to select leaders.

charter: a document or constitution for a formal organization of a corporate body.

civil war: a war between two groups in the same country.

censure: a formal statement of disapproval for one's actions.

Cherokee: a Native American tribe in Georgia, Tennessee, North Carolina, and South Carolina.

chickee: an open-sided structure with palm leaves.

Communion: a religious practice of eating and drinking blessed bread and wine.

Constitutional Convention: a group of American leaders that gathered in Philadelphia in 1787 to address issues with power in the federal government that dealt with foreign affairs and other problems.

courier: a messenger.

Creek Indian Wars: The Creek War of 1813-14; a part of the War of 1812. The Creeks were aided by England and Spain and fought General Andrew Jackson in present-day Alabama.

cutlass: a short, curved sword popular with sailors and pirates.

delegation: a group of people that represent others.

democracy: a free government where everyone has rights and privileges.

disbarred: to expel or bar from the legal profession.

dragoon: an infantryman on horseback with a short musket.

dyslexia: a visual processing problem also called word blindness that causes poor reading skills.

economic depression: a long-term drop in financial activity and gain.

electoral vote: when specially chosen voters represent their states by voting for a President and Vice President.

eulogy: a speech given at someone's funeral.

federal: the legislative (Congress), executive (President), and judicial (Supreme Court) branches of the United States government.

federalists: members of the Federalist Party who wanted a strong national government and opposed the Democratic-Republican Party.

Force Bill: a bill that forced South Carolina to obey federal laws.

First Bank of the Unites States: the first bank organized for the federal government of the United States and approved by President George Washington.

Great Father: a nickname created by critics given to President Andrew Jackson who was said to see and treat Native Americans as children.

Greek Revival Style: a Greek architectural trend of the late 18th and early 19th centuries featuring symmetrical and formal details.

House of Burgesses: the lower house of the Virginia legislature; the first legislative body created in 1619 by Jamestown colonists.

import: to bring into a country through commerce, trade, or smuggling.

impressment: forcing men into the military or navy.

inauguration: the formal admission of a man or woman into an official office or position.

infantry: foot soldiers.

King Andrew: a nickname given to President Andrew Jackson by those who felt he abused his powers of the executive branch of government.

Kitchen Cabinet: a name given to President Andrew Jackson's closest friends and unofficial advisors that came and went through the White House kitchens.

Martial Law: suspending law for a military government.

memorandum: a message, note, or record for future reference.

monopoly: controlling all of the trade or supply.

National Treasury: another name for the Department of the Treasury that manages the federal government's money.

Napoleon of the Woods: A nickname given to Andrew Jackson referring to the French military emperor, Napoleon Bonaparte, who used war to create a European empire.

neutral: choosing to not take any side or voice an opinion.

New World: a name first used for the West Indies, or Caribbean, when Columbus landed in what is today the Bahamas.

North Portico: the elaborate, tall, and covered porch of the White House that provides covered access to the Entrance Hall; added in 1830.

National Debt: the amount of money owed by the federal government.

Nullification Proclamation: a proclamation issued to South Carolina that claimed a state could not ignore or change federal law.

nullify: to declare legally invalid.

opiates: drugs that contain opium commonly used for pain.

Panic of 1819: the money crisis following the War of 1812 when banks failed and people could no longer buy or afford homes or find jobs.

Pet Banks: state banks chosen by the Treasury to receive government funds as directed by President Andrew Jackson.

Petticoat Affair: the 1830 scandal of President Jackson's Cabinet and their wives who ostracized fellow Cabinet member, John Eaton, and his young, beautiful wife, Peggy.

piracy: attacking ships at sea to rob and plunder.

Presbyterian: a religion professing forms of Christianity and Calvinism.

Principle Chief of the Cherokee: the chief executive, or president, of the Cherokee nation.

province: an area or region of a country.

Puritans: early members of the Protestant religion who split off from the Church of England to worship more simply and obediently.

Redcoats: a nickname for a British soldier.

Republicans: the rival party of the Democratic Party that opposed slavery and came to power under President Abraham Lincoln.

rheumatism: pain or stiffness in the hands, feet, or back.

rot: a disease that causes decay due to bacteria or fungi.

secession: withdrawal; to pull out; as in when states withdrew from the Union prior to the Civil War.

Second Bank of the United States: The second national private corporation that handled the finances of the U.S. Government.

Seminoles: Native Americans originally from Florida who were influenced by the Spanish and Creek Indians.

Sharp Knife: a popular nickname given to Andrew Jackson by the Creek Indians.

smallpox: a deadly, contagious disease characterized by red spots that leave scars.

solicitor: a lawyer.

South Carolina Ordinance of Nullification: a bill that nullified the Tariff of 1828 and 1832 on goods.

Specie Circular: the executive order by President Andrew Jackson that all payment for government land be in gold and silver.

Spoils System: the practice of awarding public office to political supporters.

Stamp Act: a British tax on all paper forced on American colonists so strict it included playing cards.

stock: parts of a company that can be divided for ownership.

subsidies: grants or funding; helpful free money.

sword cane: a blade for self-defense disguised as a walking stick.

tariff: a tax.

Tariff of 1824: a tax or fine created to protect industrial growth in America by taxing cheaper British goods.

Tariff of Abominations: a nickname for the Tariff of 1828 that increased the tax of the Tariff of 1824.

tenure: the possession of a term.

Texas Army: military men in Texas who served under General Sam Houston to fight for Texas independence from Mexico.

The Indian Removal Act: a law that authorized President Andrew Jackson to give land west of Mississippi to the Cherokee Nation.

The Trail of Tears: the forced migration of the Cherokee Indians to Oklahoma territory.

The War of 1812: the war between the United States and Great Britain over land and trade; also called the "Second War for Independence."

Tories: colonists who supported Great Britain during the American Revolution.

Treaty of Ghent: the treaty signed in Ghent, Belgium, that ended the War of 1812.

Treaty Party: members of the Cherokee nation who signed the Treaty of Echota in 1835 with the United States Government agreeing to surrender Georgia land.

Twelfth Amendment: details the process of electing the President of the United States.

tyrant: a dictator or bully.

veto: reject.

Whigs: an early political party created to oppose Democrats.

widower: a man who has lost a wife.

Wildcat Banks: remote, western banks with little regulation chartered under states between 1816 and 1863 in the United States.

mar: an early American Indian tribe in the Waxhaw, North Carolina area.

Index

T
Tariff of 1824: 108, 153, 160, 165
Tariff of Abominations: 108, 160, 165
tenure: 106, 160
Texas Army: 126, 160, 165
The Indian Removal Act: 9, 112, 114, 153, 160, 163, 165
The Spoils System: 105, 165
The Trail of Tears: 9, 112, 116, 138, 140–142, 154, 160, 165
the War of 1812: 67, 70, 83–84, 88–89, 116, 152, 156, 158, 160, 162, 165
Tories: 22, 24, 160, 165
Treaty of Ghent: 89, 152, 160, 165
Treaty Party: 139, 160, 165
Twelfth Amendment: 98, 160, 165
tyrant: 120, 127, 145–146, 160

W
Whigs: 120–121, 147, 160, 165
Wildcat Banks: 119, 160, 165
Wysacky: 16, 165

Bibliography

Andrew Jackson's Kitchen Cabinet. Video. **www.history.com**. Web. June 2016.

"Battle of New Orleans." www.**history.com**. A+E Networks: 2009. Web. 28 June 2016.

Black, Jason Edward. "Memories of the Alabama Creek War, 1813–1814: U.S. Governmental and Native Identities at the Horseshoe Bend National Military Park." American Indian Quarterly 33.2 (2009): 200-29. Web.

Brands. H. W. *Andrew Jackson His Life and Times*. New York: Doubleday, 2005.

Buell, Augustus C. History of Andrew Jackson, Volume 1. New York: Charles Scribner's Sons, 1904.

Cave, A. Alfred. "Life of Andrew Jackson." Journal of the Early Republic, Vol. 9, No. 2 (Summer, 1989), pp. 264–265. University of Pennsylvania Press on behalf of the Society for Historians of the Early American Republic. JSTOR. Web. 28 June 2016.

Cole, Donald B. "Honoring Andrew Jackson before All Other Living Men." Reviews in American History, Vol. 13, No. 3 (Sep., 1985), pp. 359–366. The Johns Hopkins University Press.

"Compromise Tariff of 1833." **www.american-historama.org**. Web. 28 June 2016.

Correspondence of Andrew Jackson. Vol. 1. pp. 489–492. **www.nps.gov**. Web. June 2016.

"Davy Crockett." Encyclopedia Britannica. Britannica Academic. Encyclopedia Britannica Inc., 2016. Web. 17 Jun. 2016.

Denson, Andrew. "Andrew Jackson and His Indian Wars. By Robert V. Remini. (New York Viking, 2001. Pp. xvi, 317.

"Essays About Andrew Jackson." Miller Center. University of Virginia. Web. 28 June 2016.

Glyndon G. Van Deusen. *The Jacksonian Era: 1828–1848*. New York: Harper & Brothers, 1959.

Hall, Loretta. "Creeks." **www.everyculture.com**. Web. 28 June 2016.

Haveman, Christopher D. "Weatherford, William." Academic World Book. World Book, 2016. Web. 20 June 2016.

Higgins, Rachel Loving. The Mississippi Valley Historical Review, Vol. 24, No. 1 (Jun., 1937), pp. 76–77. Oxford University Press.

Hutton, Paul Andrew. Frontier Hero Davy Crockett. Wild West. Vol. 11, Issue 5. February 1999.

"Indian Removal Act." **www.historynet.com**. Web. 28 June 2016.

"Inside the White House." **www.whitehouse.gov**. Web. 29 June 2016.

Jackson, Andrew. *Funk and Wagnalls New World Encyclopedia.* World Almanac Education Group, Inc. Funk & Wagnalls. 2014.

Jackson, Andrew. "Jackson's Defeat of the Creeks." March 28, 1814. Westward Expansion and the War of 1812, 1803–1820. By Andrew Jackson. Academic World Book. Web. 19 May 2016.

Latner, Richard B. "The Kitchen Cabinet and Andrew Jackson's Advisory System." The Journal of American History. Vol. 65, No. 2 (Sep., 1978), pp. 367–388. Oxford University Press.

"Letter from Andrew Jackson in the Hermitage to Sam Houston, March 12th, 1845." Transcribed by Danielle Brissette, Curator of Education, Sam Houston Memorial Museum. January 2014.

"Letters of General Samuel Hopkins of Henderson, Kentucky." Register of Kentucky State Historical Society 41.137 (1943): 269-303. Web.

Loyal Publication Society. "Opinions of the Early Presidents, and of the Fathers of the Republic, Upon Slavery and upon Negroes as Men and Soldiers." New York: Wm. C. Bryant Co, 1863.

"Major Participants in the Creek War." National Park Service. Web. 28 June 2016.

Marquis, James. *The Raven: A Biography of Sam Houston.* Austin: University of Texas Press, 1929.

"Maysfield Road Act." **http://historyengine.richmond.edu**. Web. 28 June 2016.

McKeehan, Wallance L. *Sons of Dewitt Colony Texas.* "The Battle of San Jacinto and the San Jacinto Campaign." **www.tamu.edu**. Web. 28 June 2016.

Pickett Albert James. *History of Alabama and incidentally of Georgia and Mississippi, from the earliest period.* Sheffield: R.C. Randolph. 1896.

Remini, Robert. V. "Andrew Jackson and the Indian Removal Act." **www.historynet. com**. 28 June 2016.

Remini, Robert V. "The Final Days and Hours in the Life of General Andrew Jackson." Tennessee Historical Quarterly 39.2 (1980): 167-77. Web.

Remini, Robert V. "Texas Must Be Ours." American Heritage Magazine. Vol 37. Issue 92. 1986.

Sellers, Charles Grier. "Andrew Jackson versus the Historians." The Mississippi Valley Historical Review 44.4 (1958): 615-34. Web.

Sherwood, Marika. "Britain, slavery and the trade in enslaved Africans." **www.history. ac.uk**. Web. 28 June 2018.

Tankersley, Kenneth Barnett. "Creek Indians." World Book Student. World Book, 2016. Web. 28 June 2016.

"Texas Independence." **www.u-s-history.com**. Web. 29 June 2016.

"The Battle of Horseshoe Bend and Its Consequences." National Park Service. Web. 28 June 2016.

"The Cabinet." **www.whitehouse.gov**. Web. 28 June 2016.

"The Conquerors." Episode 3: Andrew Jackson - Conqueror of Florida. Web. 28 June 2016.

"The South Carolina Nullification Controversy. **www.ushistory.org**. Web. June 30 2016.

"The War Against the Bank." **www.ushistory.org**. Web. June 2016.

"Timeline of the Battle of New Orleans." **http://battleofneworleans.org**. Web. 28 June 2016.

"War of 1812 - Battle of Horseshoe Bend." Tennessee State Museum. Web. 28 June 2016.

Waselkov, Gregory A., University of South Alabama. "Fort Mims Battle and Massacre." Encyclopedia of Alabama. Web. 28 June 2016.

Author Bio

Danielle Thorne is the author of seven historical and contemporary adventures and more. From pirates to presidents, she loves to research and travel while writing poetry, novels, and non-fiction. Some of her work has appeared in places like Arts and Prose Magazine, Mississippi Crow, The Nantahala Review, storySouth, and The Mid-West Review. She has co-chaired writing competitions for young authors and is active with several online author groups.

A former editor for Solstice and Desert Breeze Publishing, Mrs. Thorne keeps a blog and enjoys meeting readers and writers around the world through conferences and social media. Currently, she is working on her next piece of pirate fiction. She is a BYU-Idaho graduate, youth leader, certified diver, half-hearted runner, and unofficial foodie. She lives south of Atlanta, Georgia, with a Mr. Thorne and cat named Finnigan. Visit her at **www.daniellethorne.com**.